SURROUNDED BY HIS LOVE

Carolyn Bradley

Printed in the United States of America
Library of Congress Control Number: 2025902044
ISBN: Softcover   979-8-89518-767-8
               e-Book   979-8-89518-768-5
Published by: WP Lighthouse
Publication Date: 01/24/2025

To buy a copy of this book, please contact:
WP Lighthouse
Phone: +1-888-668-2459
support@wplighthouse.com
wplighthouse.com

In loving memory of James Majoris, my brother, who gave the world a shining example of love, hope, prayer, and caring, and for all our loved ones who likewise gave us an example of how to leave the world a better place.

TABLE OF CONTENTS

Part 2

Part 5

Part 6

ILLUSTRATIONS

PREFACE

Surrounded by his love, we are given great peace and joy, knowing he is there, with us, for all eternity. Our families, our friends, and our lives are all intertwined with his love, comfort, hope, care, and help for us and for all. We live our lives surrounded by his love.

ACKNOWLEDGMENTS

With thankfulness and deep appreciation, I would like to acknowledge all the contributors to this book:

Jeff Bradley
Bernadette Finley
Karina Garrison
Barbara Hervey
Claude Kinty
Jonathan Llewellyn
Ann Majoris
Isaac Majoris
Michael Majoris
Josie Pate
Lynda Cross Slowikowski
Sharon Ann Steele
Marilynn Walker
Margie Zellars

PART 1

"You gave me life and showed me kindness,
and in Your care, You watch over my life."

—Job 10:12

THE GREAT COMMANDMENT

Claude Kinty

"Thou shalt love the Lord God with all thy heart, and with all thy mind. This is the first and great commandment and the second is like unto it. Thou shalt love thy neighbor as thyself" (Matt. 22:37–39, KJV).

When we look at the cross of Jesus Christ, we can see the true meaning of the love of God. We know that what he did, he did for us, and he called us to walk in that love for one another.

"And above all things have fervent charity among yourselves. For charity shall cover a multitude of sins" (1 Pet. 4:8, KJV).

"If a man loves me, he will keep my words, and we will come unto him and make our abode with him" (John 14:23, KJV).

"Beloved, let us love one another, for love is of God, and everyone that loveth is born of God and knoweth God. He that loveth not, knoweth not God, for God is Love" (1 John 4:7–8, KJV).

THE OLD LIONS

Karina Garrison

I entered the hospital to visit my father the same way I left it—weary and with a tender vine of heartache weaving itself around my emotions. Saying that the recent months had been tough would be an understatement, and the last few years—well, they had been brutal. I'd been to the heights of hope only to crash and burn. I'd witnessed the kindest of hospital staff and the coldest and most insolent ones. I'd batted away "quality of life" speeches and replaced them with the true value of human life.

Everywhere I turned, it seemed there was an endless sea of hurdles to scale or mountains to move.

As an inspirational speaker and writer, my well of what I thought was never-ending inspiration was, indeed, drying up.

Even people of faith get weary, I reasoned. *So what do they do then?*

How do they draw water from an empty well?

I remembered when I held my father's hand a few days earlier. He couldn't speak or move, but his eyes found mine when I called to him.

The staff didn't think much of that fact, but I did. I recognized the flame in his blue depths—that spark of fire that showed me that he understood and was still present and pushing to survive.

The day before he'd gotten ill, he'd asked me about the writing project I'd been working on. He'd always offered me ideas, eager to help and proud of his youngest child, the author. But on this particular day, we were interrupted, and I hadn't answered his question. It has bothered me ever since; the question just hung there—lingering in the air like a leaf on an autumn breeze.

We'd been unable to communicate fully since.

"Dad," I whispered in his ear, "I want to write again—to work on something that would make you proud, but I'm really struggling. Inspiring words can't come from a dark place. I wish you could give me ideas like before."

"Are you Karina?" a nurse asked as she entered the room. "Earlier, your family mentioned you'd be in. They also told me that you're a writer."

A writer of no words, I thought. "Yes," I said.

"You currently working on anything?" she asked, and I couldn't tell whether she was truly interested or just trying to make conversation.

"Not at the moment," I answered, but even as I spoke, I grimaced.

I had never been without uplifting words before.

My father moaned as the nurse touched his sore arm, and I turned to him. Even at his advanced age, he'd been through more gut-wrenching procedures than many younger men, yet he still fought with a determined, ironclad spirit to survive.

Once again, I was reminded of his remarkable generation—of that war-veteran era that produced some of the most tenacious and faithful human beings ever. They were valiant fighters and steadfast defenders of everything decent. But how had they remained so strong? What secret did they harbor that I and the current generations could learn from?

"I'm sorry, but you'll have to leave now," the nurse instructed, drawing me out of my thoughts. "He's scheduled for more tests. You can return after seven."

I studied her for a moment. Who was this woman, really? Was she gentle? Kind? Impatient? Who were all of these medical people who were caring for my loved one?

"I'm sorry," she said again when I didn't budge, "but we must get him ready."

Swallowing hard, I laid my cheek against his—this man whose shoes I'd stepped upon and danced with as a little girl—this man who'd fought for his country with pride, watched fellow servicemen die, and continued to recount stories and acts of brave men and women who'd upheld noble principles in a time seemingly forgotten by today's society. And now he was looked upon as not much more than a sick, elderly stranger in the eyes of those caring for him. "I wish I had your strength,

Dad," I whispered in his ear. "I wish I had a vision on how I can get through these really tough times."

I had to do many difficult tasks in my life, but leaving a vulnerable loved one in the care of complete strangers was one of the hardest.

I wept as soon as I stepped outside his room.

After I pulled my car into my driveway and entered my house, I threw off my jacket and shoes, wishing it were just as easy to throw away the problems of a day.

Stepping outside to my patio, I moved a few research books on England's Kew Gardens from my chair, noticing that the wind had flipped the pages of one particular volume to a section on old trees. I put it aside and then sat down, gazing out toward the field and to an old maple tree that my father had always loved.

Throughout twenty years, I'd watched the neighborhood kids, including my own, meet there. That tree was a first for many things—from football games to first kisses. It had survived the fiercest storms and even droughts and had remained solidly rooted in spite of its age. *Just like so many of our older generation*, I thought. *Just like my father.*

As I studied the tree, I felt as if it was encouraging me to borrow some of its strength. "I need more encouragement than an old maple tree," I whispered. "A revelation would be nice."

An hour passed. Since sitting on my patio hadn't eased my heavy thoughts, I decided to get comfort food. The drive-through was chaotic due to parking-lot construction. "Just follow the old lions to get out," the cashier told me after she handed me my food and change.

"Pardon?" I asked, confused. "The old lions," she said again.

"'The old lions'? I don't understand."

"The old *lines*," she shouted, pointing to the faded yellow lines marking the pavement. "It's one-way traffic."

"Oh, I'm sorry. It sounded like you were saying 'the old lions.'"

Embarrassed, I made my way out of the lot, stopping to let an elderly couple pass as they walked to their car. The husband, sporting a Marine veteran cap, could barely walk, yet he tenderly supported his wife, protecting her from a possible fall in spite of the limits of his own fragile body.

I love this generation. I thought of my father's strong will and was also moved by this man's devotion to his wife. They were all part of a diminishing generation that America was losing more and more of every day.

"So how does one get their perseverance and true grit?" I asked aloud.

But only silence answered me, and I headed back home.

Once again, I found myself on my patio, gazing out at the old maple tree and thinking of my father and how his glory days were now fading just like the sun setting over the horizon.

Glancing at the nearby wicker table, I saw the pile of research books, and beside them was my writer's notebook; its pages currently remained blank. Nothing was written. Nothing was even started.

I picked up the volume that the wind had blown open earlier and stilled. Surely I wasn't seeing correctly. "There's no way," I whispered, but there it was—one whole section that examined five magnificent trees that were planted in 1762 and still thrived today in London. The British referred to these long-standing beacons of tenacity as *the Old Lions.*

The Old Lions. The Old Lions.

The woman at the fast-food drive-through . . . my hearing her incorrectly the Old Lions.

Suddenly, the threads of the time that I spent deliberating on my father's generation were woven together, providing the revelation I had hoped for.

Lions—the fiercest, strongest, and most respected of animals—were used throughout the ages as symbols of strength and might. It was only fitting that the trees planted in the Royal Botanic Gardens of Kew had been given that name.

But what of the trees themselves? And even the ancient maple that my father loved?

What could I and others glean from such steadfast examples of strength and character?

And so I researched deeper, learning about the Old Lions and their foundation, their roots, and how deep they grew and spread to survive the cruelest of seasons throughout the centuries.

Even the maple tree in the distance—sure, it had lost a few branches, weathered heavy storms, and survived droughts and disease, yet it still stood magnificently and proudly, remaining a beacon of perseverance.

I thought of the elderly couple I had spotted earlier—their aura of integrity—and I thought of the WWII veterans I'd known—how they'd seen the best and worst of human nature, how they'd tended to their wounded comrades—sometimes holding them in their arms as they died. Yet they went on to lead productive, giving lives. I thought of my father, who had experienced the horrors of battle but rose to the heights of victory, his fierce loyalty and pride in America evident with every nostalgic memory he recounted.

These people had lived in a time with full hardships, depression, epidemics, wars, losing children before vaccinations, and so much more.

But they'd carried on in spite of everything.

Earlier, I had wondered how people could continue pushing through life's challenges despite being weary to the core, and now I had my answer.

They simply stood and withstood.

Just like the Old Lions. And just like our current older generation.

They were one and the same.

Grabbing my purse and jacket, I rushed back to the hospital, eager to share all that I'd learned. Once I was in my father's room, I studied his face. He was paler now—most likely from whatever tests he'd gone through. His eyes were closed, but it didn't matter. I knew he could hear me. I gazed at his favorite Navy veteran ball cap, which I had placed in his view, and then I took his hand.

"I asked you to inspire me like before, and you have, Dad. Even without speaking, you've given me my story, and I'm going to tell you all about it."

"Excuse me," a new nurse said as she entered the room. She looked down at her chart. "This is Edward, correct?"

I smiled—the first time in many weeks.

"Is this Edward?" I asked her, gesturing toward my father and remembering his stories of old—his memories of the bygone, tough era that he'd struggled through to be here now. *Just like his generation had done*, I thought, *and just like his daughter will do.*

The lineage was there.

I stroked his hand gently and then turned back to the nurse. "This man is so much more than the name Edward. He's a loving father, a proud serviceman of his country, a giver to those in need, is ornery as hell, and is stronger than most who are half his age."

Bringing his hand to my lips, I kissed it.

"So you are not just caring for a man named Edward, my friend.

You are tending to one of the last, few, great Old Lions."

And then I grinned while meeting her curious eyes. I was ready to talk—ready to inspire—for I was once again a writer with words.

BLUE SHE WORE

Jeff Bradley

A grandmother creating beautiful memories with wonderful
Christmas Eve suppers for her grandson and a gift that is eternal!

The light shone all around. Blue, she wore.

A light more than all the Christmas lights combined—

More beautiful, she would be.

And as I sat, I began to wonder where all the magic had gone.

Every year was special, but the light had seemed to fade.

But tonight, I would be able to see

The hands that kneaded dough, that set the table, that wove the lights.

Two simple strands, I remember, but with hands of love,

They were magical to see.

Held together by gossamer threads, they came down from heaven unseen.

This woman who held a family together with her love—

We would all be a part of it.

But for her love, this would not be.

Christmas Eve would come—the food, the love,

The notes of a song sung into the night—

Sometimes cold, reflected back from great eyes of love,

The family would be more blessed.

And take, we would—little by little—of this woman's love.

She would give to all.

And though we took, we could not quite return this wonderful gift.

And so it would grow dim as her hand was taken

Away each year, as she grew older.

The wonder would slowly fade,

And we would search,

Not knowing where it had gone,

Until this Christmas Eve.

I saw the angel and what had brought it all to be.

Surely she had come to save us all.

And I thought just now that I might be jealous of heaven,

If that could be allowed, for the gift it would receive.

The angels would surely bow low,

As received into heaven, its raiment *more bright*.

With eyes of age, filled with love,

Working hands that spun us silver, brought us gold,

The tastes in the kitchen, the paper dolls.

Words of love, a woman of prayer,

She would bow.

And then I could see the Father.

Welcoming, he would smile

And take her love, placing her at the center.

Everything in its turn, returned—

Every gift, every prayer,

Every word lifted high.

And so seeing, all of heaven would sigh

And receive this gift.

More precious than diamonds, more beautiful than gold,

For they would all then say her name aloud.

Surely they would call her *Ann*.

YOUR FIRST DAY

Hello, Madalyn Marie! So happy to have you here on your very first day. I saw you opening your eyes to see this world that was so new to you. Did you think we would all be there to love you, to hold you, to share in your joy—your day—your very first day without being in the confines of your mother's womb?

We all looked at you and marveled—so new, so beautiful, so loved: Mom and Dad and sister Nevaeh, grandmas and grandpas, great-grandmas and great-grandpas, and cousins and friends.

We were *all* there to see *you!* Did you know this? Did you realize what was happening? We are celebrating your birthday today, and we celebrate God for giving you to all of us!

Such a gift, you are, and such a treasure. It is such a wonder to think that we never knew you or saw you before, and yet, here you are—beautiful, beloved, and so special.

We stare in wonderment at you—your perfect little fingers, your little toes, your blinking eyes—and we say,

"Thank you, God, for Madalyn Marie."

"Thank you, God, for her parents, who chose life."

"Thank you, God, for the gift of life—for us all."

Welcome to our world, little Madalyn Marie. It is now your world too.

Welcome home!

EMMA

Emma is a friend of mine—kind, caring, and sympathetic to all. She had become a licensed practical nurse, and we worked together at a nursing home for eight years.

I marveled at her sweetness of disposition in all circumstances.

She told me a story of a happening in her life. She said she was getting a divorce at the time due to her husband's wishes, and she had other family problems at the same time.

She was discouraged and depressed and felt lost and alone.

She had gone out of the house in the early-morning hours before work to take a walk, and she climbed one of the hills surrounding the city where she lived. The arid ground on the hill was hard to climb, but she kept ascending to get to the top.

There were only a few cacti there, and the vegetation was sparse. She happened to catch sight of something in one of the cacti. She looked at it more carefully and spotted a nest—a bird's nest—tucked within the bends of the cactus. There it lay with three little birds stretching their necks to see around the nest. The mother bird was not anywhere to be found, and Emma thought that she was probably looking for food to feed her brood.

Noting that there was nothing in the area that would be of sustenance to the birds, the mother bird evidently had to fly from her nest to a farther distance to find food.

Something in Emma's heart changed that day as she thought of God's wonders. Here in this place, with nothing to sustain them, were three little birds waiting for their mother to feed them and trusting that she would.

Emma said she thought of how amazing nature is and how the care of the Lord is given even unto the birds as the words came to her mind from the Bible: "Are not two sparrows sold for a farthing, yet Our Heavenly Father feeds them? Are WE not then, of more value than many sparrows?"

Hope came into her heart that morning—hope for these tiny birds and also hope for herself and her dismal situation. She knew then that her heart *could* withstand life's blows if she allowed *hope* into her heart and that *her life* was not over. There were new days and new experiences waiting for her over the horizon, and God would be there.

She came down from that hill with *hope* in her heart and the *resiliency* she needed to *continue on* and to know that a *higher power* was with her and would care for her in the way he cared for these tiny birds.

She was one of God's children, and she was not alone!

Emma weathered the storm and made a new life with her nursing career in another city, and her heart knew love, contentment, and grace—grace that came from Almighty God.

She gave me a stained-glass cross one day with these words engraved on it: "WITH GOD, ALL THINGS ARE POSSIBLE."

And so, it is!

JUST FOR A MOMENT

Ann Majoris

For me, life goes on, every hour of each dawn,
Wrapped in a mantle of sorrow and strife.
My heart is heavy for loved ones gone.
It all seems so meaningless, this sorrow, this life.

I close my eyes for a moment, hoping it will cease,
Weary with problems, heartaches, and woes.
Suddenly, my spirit is lifted with a feeling of peace,
And just for a moment, I sense that God knows.

How can this be that I can feel gladness,
My problems unsolved, my sorrow none the less?
Just for a moment, my heart has no sadness,
And I know that this life is his supreme test.

'JUST FOR A MOMENT was written by my mother, Ann Majoris about 57 years ago. I found it in her Bible, written on a piece of paper that was yellowed with age, after she had passed away at the age of one hundred. When she wrote this, she had lost her mother and a few years later, she had also lost her beloved sister, Elizabeth, "Betsey" who had passed away at the age of 37, which was a devastating loss for us all.

ISAAC'S PRAYER

Isaac Majoris

Lord Heavenly Father, please bless our world with peace,

Love, hope, joy, laughter, and freedom from jealousy.

And shall our world be filled with peace.

Amen.

HUMBLE AND BEAUTIFUL, MY DAD, THE CUSTODIAN OF OUR HEARTS

Michael Majoris

While we worked on my dad's obituary a few days ago, I was initially conflicted. How does one capture the essence of a person in a few short paragraphs? Sure, all my dad's familial roles were there—father, grandfather, brother, son, uncle, and cousin—and so were his workplace listings. But what defines the measure of a man?

My dad, Jim, was primarily an operator on the slitter, and I remember the last few years of his tenure at Weirton Steel. While overcoming cancer in the winter of 1984 and into 1985 and his ever-present mental afflictions, my dad had several periods of medical absences. As he was trying to see what work would best accommodate him, he was going to accept a bid for mill custodian. He asked me how I felt about it and if I would be ashamed as other neighborhood dads had titles like superintendent or general foreman. I really did not openly express that much with him in those days, and I honestly do not remember giving a firm answer other than shrugging my shoulders and walking away.

During my college years, I lived on campus and with my mom at her parents' residence in the summer. My dad and I no longer lived together as my parents divorced a few years earlier, so we started talking daily with phone calls. I was nineteen years old. I really did not know what to say or how to carry on a lengthy conversation with him, but he remained persistent in connecting to and building a relationship with me.

I am so very thankful and grateful that I and my dad had this second chance. We kept talking daily and finding things to share and laugh and bond over. One early point of discussion was the TV show *Quantum Leap*. We both watched nightly reruns and then called each other afterward. As the main character, Sam, time-traveled and "leaped" into the past lives of ordinary people doing extraordinary things, my dad would relate. He was particularly fond of all the nostalgic references showcased by each episode. The settings were usually in the 1950s, '60s, and '70s, and my dad would be sparked into recalling and sharing a precious memory from his own youth or young adult life, like his white 1960s Oldsmobile convertible, his days of working at Scott Lumber, or the many improvement ideas he had implemented at Weirton Steel. *Wow, he should have been the mill superintendent,* I often thought.

If I had my own opportunity to go back and visit my formative years, I know I would see it differently. Time has a way of giving one perspective and appreciation. As a child and teenager, I did not fully understand my dad. I would see him sleeping in or sitting for hours on his chair. He suffered from mental illness—most of which I was shielded from by my mom; my sister, Melissa; and my maternal grandfather, Albert. But he was so strong—even more than he would ever realize. He was extraordinary at doing ordinary things, working full-time for decades and providing my family with a wonderful home life that I will always cherish. I will thankfully never know the very depths of darkness that my dad had to endure during some severe periods in his life, and there are very few of us who ever will, but with the grace of God, he came out of it each time as a shining, bright light for all of us to see.

Condoleezza Rice wrote a book about her parents titled *Extraordinary, Ordinary People*, which I often think could have been written about Jim and Donna, my father and mother. Both of them gave so much while helping me and my sister in all the facets of our lives. They made sure that all the "little" ordinary things were taken care of so we could focus on our own dreams and goals. My dad might not have been available as much as he wanted as I was growing up, but he was there for the things that mattered the most to me.

As a father myself these days, I often recall two special memory anchors from my experiences with my dad. First, as a youth, I loved baseball and wanted to improve as an outfielder. My dad would take me to the once-vacant field behind St. Joseph's Church, which was full of high grass, and hit fly balls to me. I can still see him swinging the bat and then urging me to throw the ball back as hard as I could for accuracy and speed. I kept saying, "Are you sure? You don't have a glove." He would persist for me to release a throw, and he used his shins to stop each of the rapid-fire balls coming his way. Whenever we got home, his shins were bruised quite a bit. But in his mind, it was a beautiful thing to have helped his son. Now I often think *Bruised shins are beautiful* anytime the demands of the day leave me tired and worn; my children, Isaac and Martina, need me.

When I was ready to settle on the purchase of my first house, my dad came along to meet with the inspector and the selling homeowner. My dad was very thorough with his inquiries and concerns and sometimes kept reviewing to the point that the other two fellows rolled their eyes. My dad did not care about bruising his ego. He just wanted to ensure every detail as much as possible. In his mind, there was no such thing as a stupid or nonessential question. He was not proud enough to pretend to know something. He stayed humble and put my needs first. Today, I always think *Bruised ego, begone!* anytime I have to ask the hard or repetitive questions at work or if there is something that I need to resolve with my kids at school.

Our nightly phone calls continued as I graduated college and entered the workforce, and our relationship was no longer awkward but natural and growing. He never talked down to me. He would think things through and often pause, and I would say, "Are you still there?" and he would say, "I'm thinking!" He would offer advice and leave it there if I decided to use it and would never be forceful. He was my father and teacher. Through him, I learned how to converse and talk and listen and engage others in all kinds of topics that helped me personally and professionally. His triumph of quitting smoking entirely on his own taught me a very valuable lesson of personal accountability.

My extraordinary, ordinary parents were also my friends. The 1990s were, yes, a trying time with my mom's battle with cancer, but I believe that this brought the family closer together as we relished each moment. We had such great memories, attending sporting events, family gatherings, the birth of my two nieces—Lauren and Emilee, and even rock concerts. I'll never forget discovering a *Led Zeppelin I* in my parents' record collection. I even got these two 1960s "Weirton-suburbia hippies" to attend an AC/DC concert with me and my sister in 1996.

Yes, in darkness, there is light. With my parents divorcing at the end of the 1980s, it was challenging for each of us. But it allowed me to begin again and have a relationship with my dad. As my mom passed away in 2000, my dad was there once more as the light. He became such a strong rock as I was preparing for marriage and the start of a family. I simply could not have endured all the ups and downs of my personal life without him, and I like to think that I am a much better person and father because of him.

I am so thankful for my sister, Melissa, and her husband, Dave, for being the primary caretakers of my dad, especially with his move to Bantam Ridge in 2006. These last fifteen years gave Jim such a great sense of comfort and peace and allowed him to thrive and deepen all his relationships. Every morning, he would call his mother, Ann, who he now joins in heaven. He talked frequently with his sisters: Barbara, Carol, and Michele; his cousin Raymond; and countless neighbors and friends, and of course, he talked with me and Melissa through our daily calls. Most importantly, in these last several years, Jim grew even closer to God.

My dad recently became a regular viewer of Dr. Charles Stanley's Sunday-morning sermons, taking notes and writing down important passages on yellow note paper and keeping the special collection by his sitting chair. Each Sunday, we would have some very heartfelt discussions on life, love, trust, and faith. I had come a long way from not knowing how to talk to him. He was my father, teacher, friend, and brother in Christ.

I was with him during the last few days he stayed at home. I was moved and inspired so much by how fervently and passionately he prayed. My dad was filled with the Holy Spirit and loved and trusted God with all his heart. On his last Sunday morning at home, visibly shaken and weak, he still held a pen and was trying as hard as he could to write down the scripture messages.

I am proud to say that my dad did indeed become a custodian; he was the keeper of each of our hearts. He took what was provided to him and protected it, and he left each of us feeling renewed and in a better place spiritually and mentally each time we had a conversation with him. Maybe that is Jim's legacy—he lived fully in the present moment and was a shining light that helped others face the darkness as he himself overcame so much.

One of my dad's favorite movies was *American Graffiti*. He never fully explained why he liked it so much, and I often like to think that the appeal for him was being on the cusp of a new beginning with everything unfolding in front of him—ready for the taking. All the best to you, Dad, as you continue your journey, humble (never a bruised ego) and beautiful (no more bruised shins). You will always be our shining light and the custodian of our hearts. I love you, Dad. You were extraordinary.

A GIRL OF NINETEEN

As the girl of nineteen,
Danced in the dance hall,
He entered the door,
And saw her above all.

For all he could see,
Was a girl of nineteen,
Swaying to music,
With a sweet tambourine.

He approached her so softly,
And asked her to dance,
And thought to himself,
Could this be perchance?

The love of his life,
And the hope of his heart?
And he wished from that day,
They never would part.

He lifted softly her feet
In the air,
And she said that he said,
He always would care.

She said that he said,
She'd never grow old.
She said that he said,
His love was untold.

For the girl of nineteen,
Would be his sweet wife,
He thought to himself,
For the rest of his life.

For the love in his heart,
Blossomed that day,
And the wedding day came,
Not too far away.

And the babies, they came,
And the rocking chair rocked,
And all these memories,
Were in their hearts, locked.

And the children, they grew,

So straight and tall,

And the years drifted by,

With them loving them all.

Then came the middle years,

Autumn's slow step.

She was a grandma,

And like babies, they slept,

Right in her arms,

On an old rocking chair,

And she said that he said,

Her face was still fair.

Then came the silver threads,

Binding the gold.

Hands were unsteady,

But she never grew old.

For that girl of nineteen,

Still lived in his heart,

And she said that he said,

They never would part.

She walked more slowly,

And he saw her there,

A girl of "nineteen,"
On an old rocking chair.

Then one day, it came,
That the rocking chair sat,
Still and forlorn,
With just an old man's hat,

Crowning the top,
Of the spindles so fair,
And he couldn't bring himself
To sit in her chair.

For she went ahead
To make him a place,
So cozy and warm,
Filled with heaven's dear grace.

And there she would wait,
That fair girl of nineteen,
Waiting to see him,
Holding her sweet tambourine.

CHANGE

Perhaps some of the dreams we try to save are well spent and worn,
and perhaps they need to be changed into something new,
different, and unafraid.
Perhaps the things we cling to had their day
and gave the loveliness within for our hearts to know
that they were part of a bigger picture, a larger clime,
where all dreams can go—both new and old.
Perhaps there is a time to set aside the ones from before
and go to the ones who are, this day,

knocking at our door.

Perhaps our foolish hearts that seek to block all change

can regroup and say

"What was lovely was lovely in its day,

but I can part with it to expand my view,

to set out on new horizons and new moons,

and to make the world feel the glow of a new dream,

envisioned on the horizon,

and a new hope—to set my spirit free,

not to be encumbered by a myriad of things

but to go loosely on my way and finding hope—

find everything!"

HELPING WITH PTSD

PTSD (posttraumatic stress disorder): Many people have it; I do too. I had gone through a psychiatric admission to a hospital's floor. It was due to an abnormal thyroid level, which I didn't know at the time. I pray that those who exhibit psychiatric symptoms all have their thyroid levels checked.

After I had come home, I was better with all the symptoms, but I did have PTSD due to the trauma of being in the hospital for a month and all the terrible things that had happened due to my confusion. I had gotten better with the proper treatment of an increased amount of thyroid medication each day.

PTSD brings all the thoughts, experiences, and trials back into the mind, and you have to keep battling the thoughts, the happenings, and the terror of it all.

I have found that we have a remedy in *Jesus*, who we can see as being there—*with us*—even though we couldn't see or feel him at the time. Perhaps we even gave up on God, but he didn't give up on us. He promises to be with us all the time. So he *was* there. We can know that he did *not* leave us.

Perhaps he sent a friend, a family member, or someone else to give us support.

For soldiers on the battlefields, you can picture Jesus there, looking at you and helping you in many ways. Jesus *never* forsakes us, and so he is with us *through* it all.

Praise is a key to *healing* if we can *praise* God for the happenings.

Father, I praise you for everything—for all the things that happened

in my life and for the gift of *you* and for sending help for me.

And, if you can, say "I praise you, Father, for everything in my life.

Amen." There is a breakthrough.

If you have been to war, see *Jesus* there, lying on the ground with you, walking where you were walking—beside you everywhere. He was there, looking, watching, waiting—*helping*.

Even though we didn't see him, feel him, or understand *how* he was helping us, we can *know that he was and is now in our PTSD*.

The worst thing we can do is despair and not want to live anymore. God has a plan that will get us through the PTSD so that we can get well and then can bless others.

Sometimes the best thing to do is to tell others about our experiences and to *keep telling* the story whenever the occasion arises

---

and *then put it to rest.* Then, there comes a time when we can change our thoughts— change our thoughts and *not* think or relive them anymore. There comes a time to *stop* and think of *other* things—the *good* memories and the *wonderful happenings* in our lives.

We *can relive* those memories of riding bicycles, playing ball, and in my case, playing with paper dolls and coloring in coloring books when I was young. We can enjoy all the wonderful memories that we made as we saw our children, grandchildren, and even great-grandchildren growing up. There is a way to *change* the majority of our thoughts along these lines.

When a traumatic thought will still enter, we can say, "It's over. It's done. I don't have to relive it anymore. I don't have to have the fear, horror, and terror in my heart anymore, for it is *done—finished—*like water going under a bridge and moving on, not staying under the bridge and its darkness."

We can be free, and it is very healing to engage in activities throughout our days. I like to write books, so I enjoy getting them all together. I like to paint pictures and to color still with the wonderful Crayola crayons. I enjoy watching light romantic movies on television and listening to the religious programs that I find on different channels.

I like to pray—to give God my day—first thing in the morning and then say different prayers throughout the day. I like to read the Word of God, the Bible. We should never let one day go by without opening the Bible and reading the words of God that will bring *life* to our souls. God's Word has the power to heal, to comfort, to enlighten, and to save us. There *is* salvation in the Bible, and a good suggestion from many people is to *memorize* his holy Word every day.

We can write a line of scripture down and place it in a place where we will see it throughout the day.

For example, you can use the following:

"You make me strong and happy Lord" (1 Sam. 2:1, CEV).

"So, REJOICE IN THE LORD, and be glad, all you who obey Him!" (Ps. 32:11, NLT).

"DO NOT be grieved, for the JOY of the LORD is your strength" (Neh. 8:10, ESV).

Changing our thoughts changes the PTSD, and if we can, we should do this: "Think on those things that are lovely, of good report, worthy of Praise—think on THOSE things and the God of Peace will be with you."

Pray, *memorize*, and *think* on those things that give our minds happiness, rest, and peace, and the *posttraumatic stress disorder* will leave.

It is in the past, and the present and future *are ahead*, with us *giving to others, loving others, and living life with God*, which will eventually bring us to the shores of eternity so that we will *live with God forever*!

I pray my prayers of hope for you and love for you and joy for you as you walk away from the darkness and put your faith in the *light of God's love*.

God's blessings to all!

"THEN THEY CRIED TO THE LORD IN THEIR TROUBLE, AND HE DELIVERED THEM FROM THEIR DISTRESS. HE SENT OUT HIS WORD AND HEALED THEM AND DELIVERED THEM FROM THEIR DESTRUCTION" (Ps. 107:19–20, ESV).

"FOR GOD DID NOT APPOINT US TO SUFFER WRATH BUT TO RECEIVE SALVATION THROUGH OUR LORD, JESUS CHRIST" (1 Thess. 5:9, NIV).

"THE LORD GOD WHO SAVES THEM, WILL BLESS AND REWARD THEM" (Ps. 24:5, CEV).

ROBE OF COMPASSION

Sharon Ann Steele

Some verses in the Bible seem so simple.

"The Lord's compassion is new every morning" (Lam. 3:22).

Seven words, one sentence. But after reading it, I found a question arising: How *can* the Lord's compassion be *new* every morning? It isn't old. It doesn't change. His compassion doesn't stop and start, so how can his compassion be *new* every morning? He is the Almighty, the unchanging God.

My mind shifted from the Lord's compassion to this part of the sentence, "is new every morning," and then went to the thought of "new mornings." I thought of how each morning begins with the same process of getting dressed. Sometimes I look out the window to see what the weather is or I dress according to my plans for the day. But in all situations, my vision is limited as I cannot see past the moment.

My mind returned to the word of God as I compared God's compassion being new every morning to my morning ritual of getting dressed, and I saw similarities. I dress myself as to what I feel would be best for the day. If the day is rainy, I bring an umbrella. If it's sunny, I bring sunglasses. If it's chilly, I bring a jacket. If I have meetings at work, I bring dress clothes, and so on.

Well, the Father does the same. For instance, there were days when my Father clothed me in a fleece robe of soft compassion to cushion my falls and to comfort my hurts. There were days when he encircled a halo of compassion around my head to calm my thoughts, or he provided a blanket of compassion to warm me in times of cold suffering. He dressed me with his compassion anew every morning according to what he knows will best meet my needs for the day. One last question entered my mind:

"What about me? What about *my* compassion for others?"

Perhaps, I too, even though I possess a limited vision, must look at others with new compassion every day. I do believe that the compassion that God gives to me is not for me to keep but for me to experience, learn from, be thankful for, and pass on.

God's word warmed my heart. The Lord's compassion *is new every morning*. He is a God of love who custom-fits his garments of compassion for me so that they meet my daily needs.

HATS

In my husband's closet, on the top shelf, are many hats—mostly baseball hats. There are sixteen Pittsburgh Pirates hats—with the letter P across the middle—in various colors and one of them green and one red and black, two postseason Pirates hats, eight Pittsburgh Penguins hats, and two Pittsburgh Penguins Stanley Cup champion hats, showing 2009 and 2016. There are also two Wheeling Nailers hats and two hats from Marco Island, gifts from our daughter, that are all stacked on the shelf, among others. I have asked Dave, my husband, if he would like to dispose of any of them, and the answer is "*No.* They have good memories."

Dave is a master of life and has always given his best to whatever he does. His devotion to the Pittsburgh Pirates baseball team stems from when he was six years old—when his family were fans—and it has never wavered. He was a Pittsburgh Penguins ice-hockey team fan before many in our area even knew of the Penguins, and Dave would attend many games with his children, family, and friends.

He is a master of hats, wearing not only real hats on his head but also supernatural hats of kindness, forgiveness, love, devotion, and a quiet presence about him when things aren't going so well.

Dave has Parkinson's disease now and has had it for about three years. While talking to him, you would never know it except for some hand tremors that are noticeable. He discounts having the disease, as to him, as he says, "There are much worse things that I could have."

It is not to discount those who have Parkinson's disease but his way of thinking about it in a positive way.

Dave loves dogs, and we have had six of them in our married life. He has a special bond to them, and they love him, and he loves them with devotion, love, and care. He loves to have them sit with him, and that is their time of specialness and sharing their time together.

He is a master at being a dad as he has raised our three children up with good morals, compassion, caring, and thankfulness for life itself. He was always there for them in their "growing up" years, and the children, now grown, always send him cards that say "To the Best Dad We Could Ever Have."

His wisdom is solid and knowledgeable, and he believes that any problem has an honest and well-thought-out answer.

I wonder what "hat" Dave will wear in heaven. I am sure that it will say, "Well done, good and faithful servant."

Well done, Dave! Well done!

A grandson in rehab and a letter of love.

A LETTER FROM A GRANDSON

Dear Grandma,

I got three cards from you, and I love them all.
Thank you so much. I love you and miss you. I'm doing
so good here. God has changed my life and my heart. I
have read the New Testament—all of it. Wow! That's
all that I can say. I have learned so much about myself
through God—that we are put on this earth to praise
God and give him all the glory for what we do. We are
to live for others, not ourselves. I have learned what

it means to love. God has put that in my heart and changed me completely.

Just like it says in 2 Corinthians 5:17, he makes you new, and everything in the past is gone. Amazing! That's what I feel like. I can say that I never in my life thought that God had anything for me, and the truth is, I didn't want it. You and Mom were always telling me how great he is, and I just didn't see it, but now I do. Just like it says, "For I was blind, but now, I see."

God opened my eyes to what is good in life and what it means to live. I thank God every day for what he did for me because I know I didn't deserve it, but he did it because he loves me. I thank him for you and the great family he blessed me with. I could never ask for a better one. You all have always loved me and were there when I needed you. Thank you from my heart. I love you all so much and can't wait to see you all and talk about Jesus. My favorite books in the Bible are John and 1 John because they are about love. Write me back soon, and send me some Bible verses that you like.

Love,

Your Grandson

A WINTER'S MORNING

Jeff Bradley

Sunshine this morning
And the cold
Wrapped around
Blankets of snow
Resting soft on
Houses deep.
Smoke rises in
The air, house
After house,
Looking through

A winter's haze.
The top of the
Ridge burns with
Ice fire.
The trees appear
As silhouettes
Against a winter
Blue sky.
A winter's morning to keep
You inside
And stare out in
Wide wonder
From the comfort
Of a fire's glow.
The cold right
Outside the
Window.
And all the questions and
Concerns, they
Would find their answer
Certainly if they
Would turn to Him.
I like to imagine
That they are all
For the common good
And their desires,
Well-intended.

I imagine some
Sitting down to
Breakfast,
Some sad and
Lonely, some
Praying—
All surrounded by
This cold and
Snowy tapestry
That keeps them
There, contained.
The footsteps
Blanketed the
Earth as such
Two thousand
Years ago—all for
This to remain.
And, given this
Chance, this
Freedom to do
What they would,
Each and every day—
Would they take
A moment to see
The contrast and
Beauty of a dark
Solitary Evergreen

Iced with snow
Against this sky
Of frigid blue?
Would they stop
And thank him
For the morning's gift?
The beauty, dark
And bright,
Surrounded by all
The colors of the Sun.
The blue, as his Blood,
Forever changed
By the scars
And this love,
That was sent for
You and me.

A TIME TO BE GIVEN

Grace, hope, truth, and love—

We are all given these gifts as we respond in love to God and to others.

As we seek, we will find.

As we love, we are blessed, protected, comforted, and made whole.

We are given our time on earth to learn, to grow, and to accomplish our purpose in life,

Our dreams in life, our dreams for others.

God gives us grace for our tasks and help in our daily work.

Our God Almighty also gives us a place to go to himself,

For in his presence, we all will find a place of friendship, peace, and love.

There is no safe place on earth without God.

He is our safety, our rest, our comfort, our help, our hope

In all of life's situations and happenings.

And so, we are given joy to accompany us in full measure.

On our journey, we are given the tools that we need to awaken in us truth, obedience, sacrifice, blessedness, learning, and respect

So that we may be cured and be able to help cure others.

God uses all situations to cure us of the things of our past, present, and future.

We are cured to make a difference and to give our lives in a unique way to the service of others.

You and I are partners in this journey.

We give as we have been given.

We give back to the Creator all that has gone before.

For he is light, he is love, and he forsakes none who seek him.

He is there for me and for you in all our situations.

He gives, and we are given all that we will ever need for all our lives.

Amen!

TO BREATHE THE FRESH AIR

I would like to tell you that if you have any relatives that are hospitalized for mental issues, maybe they can be checked for thyroid- hormone imbalances. Great mental confusion can be caused by a high level of thyroid-stimulating hormone (TSH). I had a terrible experience when my thyroid level was very high. I was mentally confused and had to be hospitalized on a psychiatric floor. I didn't know what was wrong with me, but I was not thinking properly, and the psychiatrist did not know what could help me. He was treating me for psychosis and even suggested shock treatments as I was not responding to the medication that he had prescribed. Luckily for me, my endocrinologist called my psychiatrist; since he knew me for many years, he knew that the problem had to be my thyroid level, which was causing myxedema madness.

I was very fortunate as my psychiatrist told me that at first, he did not believe my endocrinologist, but he did consent to getting my level and to having my thyroid medicine increased. It took a while to get the level to a normal value, but finally, I did show improvement. I was in the hospital for a month, and the doors were kept locked, of course, and the windows were sealed shut. It felt like there was no air—no fresh air to breathe—and I would look out the windows and look at the people on the street, who were so happily walking by, and some were just sitting on the curbside, and I would think of how wonderful it was to smell fresh air and to be allowed to be outside.

One of the symptoms of a high TSH level is not being able to sleep, and this happened to me. I don't know how many nights I didn't sleep. Later, I found out that there were three other women with similar symptoms, and they couldn't sleep also, and it was due to their thyroid levels.

I had also taken a lot of antibiotics before this happened because my teeth were hurting, and I don't know if that is what caused the abnormal thyroid level.

I am writing this to try to help family members that you may have who have been diagnosed with mental illness and who may get well with adjustments to their thyroid levels. I pray that they can be helped! The thyroid medication has to be taken first thing in the morning—without any other pills—and then one has to wait for half an hour to one hour before eating breakfast. After that, any other pills can be taken.

My family gave me much support through their own research and their numerous calls, visits, and prayers, and my friends gave me a lot of support as well. I can never repay them for all their love, kindness, and hard work. I will never forget the day when they told me that I would be released at the end of that week. I couldn't believe what I was hearing as I had no idea how long I would have to stay. I thought it would be much longer. I have to praise God and thank him with all my heart that I was released and got better and I escaped being institutionalized for the rest of my life. Also, I thank God for the dear endocrinologist, who took the initiative to call my psychiatrist and tell him what he thought. He told him not to do anything else with me as he was sure that it was myxedema madness and that it would clear up with the increase in thyroid medication. My endocrinologist was Dr. Sean Nolan, and I can never thank him enough for saving me. Dr. Sean passed away about nine months after he saved me. I can only say a prayer of thanksgiving to God for what he did for me and pray that his work can help others also. I know there is a special place in heaven for Dr. Sean Nolan, and I was so fortunate to have him in my life. Because of him and my family, *I can breathe the fresh air*!

LIVING WITH THE HOLY SPIRIT

I heard a Bible verse spoken on a television program: "You are no longer ruled by your desires, but by God's Spirit who lives in you" (Rom. 8:9, CEV). I had heard that verse before many times, but for some reason, it spoke deeply to my heart then. The Holy Spirit *lives in us*, and we are no longer "ruled by our desires." Romans 8:6 (CEV) states, "If our minds are ruled by our desires, we will die, but if our minds are ruled by the Spirit, we will have life and peace." I think that we sometimes go through life while not *realizing* to the fullest extent that *we are temples of the Holy Spirit*. Our bodies are Spirit-filled, and the Holy Spirit chooses to dwell in us in a way that we don't quite understand but *know that is true*.

Jesus said, "I will send you the Comforter, Who will be WITH YOU AND IN YOU."

How, then, should we take *care* of these bodies that are filled with the Holy Spirit?

We should be cautious of tainting our bodies, which are inhabited by the Holy Spirit, by telling lies, having lustful thoughts, or accepting angry thoughts, bitterness, and unforgiving thoughts and a myriad of sins that would dishonor the Holy Spirit.

If we are tempted to do these things, our thoughts should be centered on the Spirit of God. How *can* we do these things?

When we are tempted to respond in anger or bitterness toward someone, these thoughts should take precedence:

"My body is a temple of the Holy Spirit. How *can I do* these things?

Why do I want to grieve the Holy Spirit by sinning?"

"We don't fully understand the meaning of all these *words*, but *Jesus said it, and it is so.*

"*Guard* the Holy Spirit."

We should adorn our bodies, the temples of the Holy Spirit, by thinking beautiful, kind, loving thoughts, speaking such words, and doing such actions, refusing to lash out in anger, hatred, or revenge. Each of us has the responsibility to guard the temple of God within each of us with our joy, our trust, and our love of God.

God is three divine persons in one. *We love all three in our hearts, minds, and spirits.*

"Thank you, God, for this gift of the Holy Spirit in our bodies, minds, and spirits. Help us live rightfully and recognize that we are truly temples of the Holy Spirit. Amen."

THE GIFT OF LOVE

Bernadette Finley

February is the month of love, and we celebrate Valentine's Day every year. Love is the heart and soul of our lives. We need to open ourselves to the mystery of God's love in our lives. We need to act on that love in whatever ways God may lead us.

The demands of living can be hard with humiliations, misunderstandings, strained relationships, and uncertainties about the future. Sometimes it is hard to handle these personal problems, and we should commit ourselves to the Lord by putting our trust in him.

God wants our hearts. He wants us to be so identified with him— so filled with love for him—that our joy derives from belonging to him— whatever the circumstances may be.

We too are able to share our faith with our families and friends and show them how our hearts are open to God's presence and action in our lives. We need to strive to walk in the footsteps of the Lord. We will always experience joys, challenges, and disappointments, but by placing our hearts of trust in the Lord, he can help us overcome our fears and problems. Our Lord never leaves us. He knows our needs better than we do ourselves. He loves us more than we could ever imagine in this world. What an awesome thought to know that we are loved so much that he will never leave us—even in our darkest moments.

We need to trust that the Father holds our situations in his hands and he will turn them into blessings.

No matter what is happening to us, in the midst of our difficulties, God is standing there with outstretched arms, saying, "Come. Follow me."

Most importantly, God is greater than anything in our lives—our disappointments, our hopes, our dreams, our families' difficulties, our friends' problems, and our heartaches and sufferings.

God knows everything. God is great! Each day, we should thank him for this beautiful gift of love that he has given us.

As we focus more on God and less on our troubles, God will bring us into a deeper and new relationship with him. We will become *new people* if we let God's gracious gift of his own life soak into us and change our ways of thinking and fill us with his love, for *God is love!*

MAX

Max is a beagle of ours. He came to us as a puppy of four days old. His mother did not have enough milk for her brood, so my husband and I became parents for Max and his sister, Clover.

We had to feed the puppies every two hours for the first few weeks so they would survive, and we had to keep them warm and dry. It was an around-the-clock task, but we loved seeing them grow stronger each day.

We became so attached to them that we could never have parted with them. So they became a permanent part of our family, and we loved them.

When Max was six months old, he ran out the front door one day, which had been mistakenly left open, and he started up the hill toward the woods. I ran out the door and called out to him, and he looked back at me—looked me straight in the eye—and then kept running as fast as he could into the woods.

I was devastated, and my heart broke as I knew the dangers that he was facing. I knew that if he came upon a rabbit or a deer, he would probably chase them for a very long time and get farther and farther away from home and maybe not even come home.

My grandson joined me in the search, and we hurried through the woods; we called out his name but to no avail. As time passed, I became even more despondent; it would soon be dark. Another danger that Max was facing was that the woods bordered the main road on the other side, and Max was unaware of the danger of being hit by a passing car. My face was wet with tears, and I kept praying that we would find him.

It seemed like hours had passed when I glanced through a small clearing in the woods, and there was Max. His head was erect, his shoulders were back, and his eyes were looking right at me.

I ran to him, crying and laughing at the same time, and put my arms around his neck and hugged him as my tears fell on his face.

He was safe!

It reminded me of the parable of the prodigal son. The father, who was watching and waiting for his son to come home, ran to him with outstretched arms, forgiving all that he had done.

"But when he was still a great way off, his father saw him and had compassion on him, and ran and fell on his neck and kissed him" (Luke 15:20, NKJV).

We are *all* God's children. God loves us, wants to take care of us, and desires the best for us. Sometimes we may wander off, searching for things that we think will make us happy without God. When we do this, he waits and looks and wonders when we will come home to his safety, his protection, and his love.

We cannot fathom the Father's love and his joy when we return home. I got a taste of that when I first saw Max finally coming through the woods. I couldn't believe what I was seeing, and then my heart leaped for joy.

The Father's heart leaps for joy for *each one of us* when we come back to him. The Father's love is so great, so powerful, and so all-encompassing that he wants *every soul* to be safe in his arms forever.

The father waits for each one of us. All that we have to do is come home.

FROST

One morning, when a heavy frost lay on the ground, I was walking our dog in the yard and noticed that the places where the sun had been able to shine were no longer covered with the frost. The only places that still contained the frost were those that were in the shadows.

I thought of how we could all be tempted to remain in the shadows in our lives as our lives take on many turns. If we cling to bitterness, revenge, our self-will and not God's will, self-pity, despondency, despair, and our refusal to forgive, we are choosing to stay in the shadows. We are refusing to allow the warmth of God's healing love to become like a fire in our hearts, healing all the cold places within. Shadows take on many forms, and the icy tentacles—such as envy, greed, hatred, and jealousy—wrap themselves around our hearts.

To be free, we need to step out of these shadows through a conscious act of our will and allow ourselves to feel the warmth and love of God permeating our very beings. We need to *allow* the frost to melt, which will bring strength and healing for ourselves and those around us.

The frost leaves us clinging tenaciously to those things that should not be in our lives and that are destroying our happiness.

All that we need to do is step out into the sunshine with the love, peace, and forgiveness of God!

CHASING BUTTERFLIES

Michael Majoris

I am trying to keep up with my children as they cross a wooden bridge over a small stream. It is a pleasant midsummer afternoon as we trek through a few paths under the shade of many trees. We soon reach our destination—the local butterfly house and garden.

The butterflies are as plentiful as they are diverse, and my son and daughter are incredibly eager to interact with the winged insects, each grabbing two swab sticks of sugar water. A short time passes, and we are joined by several exuberant children and picture-happy parents like me. Convinced long ago that my children definitely take after their mother with their outgoing personalities, my daughter quickly has two or three new "best friends" with whom she is competing to see who can hold the most butterflies at one time. Meanwhile, my son is more interested in taking a leadership role; he instructs the younger participants on all the butterfly types and how to properly use the microscope slides. Perhaps mildly impressed by his enthusiasm, one of the two caretakers graciously hands us a net and offers us the opportunity to try and retrieve a few of the butterflies who managed to fly past the screen-door opening and into the sunlit flower bushes.

My son and I spend some time first, each taking a turn. We spot a few of the vivid flying creatures, wait for one of them to pause for some nectar, and then try and approach gently. Mostly, we are left standing without a single raise of the net as the so-called hunted is very quick and floats above to another plant. My daughter, not wanting to be left out, soon runs outside to join us and immediately wants her chance to grasp at nature's beauty. After a few minutes, I did manage to corral one into the top of the opening but had neither the skill nor the knowledge to properly secure the netting. Afraid of injuring one of my new companions, I let it go. Instead, I return to my camera, excited to take advantage of the natural sunlight, and I begin photographing candid shots of my own "butterflies," who are flittering about in a zigzag pattern.

I soon recall the pictures from our escapade here last year, and my first thought is that my girl no longer fits into her pretty blue butterfly T-shirt, although she is determined to maintain a full wardrobe of kittens, unicorns, and yes, butterflies. Her new red one suits her just fine for today. But again, the feelings of years gone by emerge—as if breaking through a cocoon. What happened to all of those days at six or seven months old—when I got to watch firsthand my little crawling caterpillar?

We decide to venture back inside the butterfly house, and I am content to just sit and absorb all of the action without the use of a digital lens, instead taking time to collect several thoughts and to further immerse myself in a few of the butterfly books on hand. Most of the collection is scientific-based, with a full listing of Latin-derived names that I cannot pronounce nor remember later, and the geographic locations are detailed. I find myself wanting to learn something unique, so I flip back to the first summary pages and read about the butterflies' special visual awareness. They can see in expanded directions and even see in ultraviolet light. Now I am fully certain that I never had a chance with the net despite my strong belief today that I am seeing more—perhaps going through my own metamorphosis.

I keep sifting through the books, searching for more personal passages, which describe the wide appeal of the butterfly. Yes, there are the brilliant arrays of color, but what I can clearly conclude is that the life of the butterfly itself is the most fascinating aspect to people. The cycle from egg to caterpillar to chrysalis to flying insect is as remarkable as it is short.

My focus is again on my children as they continue to smile and laugh with the same steadfastness as a butterfly's pursuit to pollenate flowers. Ironically, with my contemplative mindset, I watch a question-mark butterfly land on a nearby plant, and the similarities start to burgeon. Childhood is indeed very brief—from a curious infant always reaching and clutching to a toddler speaking, asking, and commenting on all topics to later years and that sweet fusion of innocence and trust with the main desire to seek out all that is fun and good. Yes, I do believe that, as with butterflies, children too can see differently—much differently than adults. I may only be able to momentarily catch a butterfly in the top of a net, and in most cases, as my kids explore their world with an unfathomable zest, the best I can do while trying as a parent who wants to always keep them safe is just manage a small tug on their shirt sleeve as they run ahead of me.

We all fondly recall many bits of our own childhoods, and who does not say, "Hey, look at that butterfly"? So why are both so precious and gentle and so very fleeting? Is it all part of God's plan to have such a heavenly living presence in our midst—so that we adults are humbled and reminded of how beautiful and simple life can be when we see the world through the eyes of a child? Mark 10:15 states, "I tell you the truth, anyone who doesn't receive the Kingdom of God like a child will never enter it." Today, I was led into a wonderful place of nature by my children, and I exit the same way, hoping to follow their rich love of life.

I may no longer have that same boundless flow of excitement that I had as a boy, and I honestly do not know when it went away or if my son will lose it too as he approaches his teen years. All I can do is hope that I can continue to stop and notice a passing butterfly, taking time to embrace the present while chasing memories from long ago.

A TIME OF PRAISE

We need to praise God, for he is worthy of all praise.

God's work is done in us each time,

As we praise him for the situations we are encountering.

To praise God is to offer him his due.

God is worthy of our love. Our cry goes up to God.

And our praise reaches the heavens. God is not a lonely God.

But he is filled up with our praises.

We let our praises ascend before his throne,

And these praises are stored in his heart.

He is worthy to be praised.

He is worthy to be loved, honored, and adored,

Throughout all the ages.

Praise is our gift to God.

That becomes a gift to us also.

Then, let us praise!

"All power belongs to you, oh Lord.

All praise belongs to you.

You are the Creator of *all*.–

You are worthy of all our praise *forever*!"

Amen!

OUR GARDEN

There is a sweetness that comes from our thoughts that are lovely on the earth,

That erases the soul of bitterness and the rhyme of discord, unforgiveness, and revenge,

To place within our hearts a treasured clime,

To have a *peaceful* garden in our minds.

To see that all is lost within ourselves

When we treasure thoughts of discord and ill will,

For it is a poison to ourselves that it becomes.

For it is a blight into our garden that it becomes,

Destroying blooms and crushing them within.

No happiness can be when poison seeks its realm,

To cloud our minds with its spew of sin,

For all deserve a rightful mind to think,

And *what we think*

Either kills or makes things grow.

Oh, if we saw how wicked are our thoughts,

Of even harboring a grudge and not letting go—

Our garden becomes hardened and sparse,

Where beauty, love, and friendship cannot grow.

So step back and see—

What is in my garden for today?

Rid it of all bitterness, unforgiveness, *and* thoughts of ill will

And make it beautiful

By choosing to forgive and let go,

And the blossoms will come

To beautify *your soul*,

And the flowers will be abundant and free.

Amen!

HAIKU FOR THE HOURS

Josie Pate

Dawn

To this new day of promise
Opportunity

Day

How to be today
Live each moment well, fully
Be in the moment

Evening

Letting go for what?
To make room for new order
For newfound freedom

Night

Be perfectly still
And know that I am God
Be perfectly still

ACCEPTING APPLICATIONS

Margie Zellars

"My son pay attention to what I say! Listen closely to my words. Do not let them out of your sight. Keep them within your heart for they are life to those who find them and health to a man's whole body" (Prov. 4:20–22, NIV).

We all have a story to tell. My friend Carol's story is one that I want to share as it has a profound message of hope and faith.

As I was leaving work one day, Carol came over to me and asked for prayers as she had some blood work done to check her cancer markers.

Carol had two previous battles with cancer and emerged from the battles as a survivor. We prayed together, and I headed home.

The next morning, I received a phone call from Carol; she told me the results were not good and asked me if I could come over and pray with her. When I got to her home, her daughter, granddaughter, husband, and pastor were there. She told us that she had put in an application to work for Jesus and that this cancer was not going to stop her. Her blood-work result was 267, and the normal value is 35. She knew from her previous battles with cancer that this was not good at all.

So many conversations and prayers went on that morning. So much of it is now a blur, but one thing that I remember is seeing many God sightings that day. Amid the confusion, emotions, and conversations, Carol remembered that we had planned to go to a healing mass at a church in Pennsylvania at 6:00 p.m. the next evening. She wanted to go to this service, but the hospital had scheduled her scan for 4:30 p.m. She was very sad that she wouldn't be able to make it to the mass. Her daughter called the scheduling department to try to rearrange the scan but was met with resistance from the nurse on the phone until she told her that her mother wanted to go to a healing service that evening. The nurse asked her to wait a minute and came back to the phone and told her the scan had been rescheduled to 9:00 a.m. Carol was ecstatic. I knew immediately that God had made this possible. This was a God sighting!

Carol had her scan the next morning, and then, in the evening, she went to dinner with me and four of her friends. One of her friends spoke to Carol about the importance of having forgiveness in her heart. Carol listened intently and took the words to heart.

At the church, Carol got down on her knees and poured her heart out to Jesus. She told us that she prayed that her heart would be opened and that all unforgiveness and sin would be purged from her heart. The priest talked about how seriously we must take our prayers and mean what we say and not take them lightly. He explained that this service was very special and holy and that we should understand that before we took part in it. He did an examination of conscience as part of the mass. One of the questions he asked was "Is there anyone you are angry with, or do you have any unforgiveness in your heart?" If there was, he asked you to let it go and give it to God. He asked many other questions, but that particular one touched Carol deeply. This was the same subject that she and her friend had spoken of during dinner and was exactly what she had prayed.

After the mass, the priest said that anyone who wished for a prayer and a blessing should come forward. Carol was among the first to go forward, and when the priest prayed for her, she was slain in the spirit. As she fell backward, the usher gently laid her down on the floor. When Carol got up, she was wobbly but so serene. Her face showed a tranquility and peace that had not been there before, and she looked like an angel to us. While riding home in the car, I believed in my heart that she had been healed.

The results of the scan were even worse than we imagined. She had a grapefruit-sized tumor on a wall of her uterus. The cancer had spread to her spleen, and there were three tumors in her liver. The doctor gave her three months to live without chemo, and even with treatment, the time left was undeterminable. Carol's husband and daughter did not tell her the limited amount of time the doctor said but told her it was stage-four cancer. Carol said it dawned on her over the weekend that things were not good when her son and his family came in from Florida and her granddaughter came in from the Navy. When her daughter called to tell me the results of the scan, I was saddened, but in my heart, I believed that Carol received healing at the service. I just knew she was healed.

There were so many other events that occurred over the following days and weeks. Carol and her husband went to her Presbyterian church one Sunday, and her pastor called them both forward during the service, and the entire congregation laid hands on them and prayed for healing. Both Carol and her husband felt heat going through their bodies during the prayer. Carol so appreciates and loves her church family and the prayers, love, kindness, and support they always give to her and her family. She said that is one of the moments she will treasure forever.

Carol decided to follow the doctor's suggestion of a series of chemotherapy treatments. She told God that she signed up for this journey and would do whatever she felt God wanted her to do to be healed. The day before her first treatment, Carol got anxious, knowing how sick she would be. She had been through this before and was not looking forward to going through it again. She wanted to be out there, telling everyone about Jesus and how he loves them. We call Carol "God's cheerleader." She prayed that God would give her peace for this journey and take away her anxiety. I called friends who are in ministry and asked if they could come with me and pray with Carol. We went to her home, and she said she had asked God to send her someone to pray with her, and this was an answer to her prayer.

Our friends also called a pastor friend of theirs in California, and from his car in a parking lot, he prayed with us and shared healing scriptures. It was such a godsend. Carol said that this helped her prepare for the morning's treatment. She felt peace.

She had her first and second treatments, but after the second treatment, she had an allergic reaction. They called in the paramedics and transported her to the emergency room at the hospital. The allergic reaction led the doctors to discover a blood clot in her lung. Had she not had the allergic reaction, the doctors would not have found the blood clot immediately, and it could have killed her. God does work in mysterious ways, and once again, another God sighting was found in her story. She was admitted to the hospital for testing and to treat the blood clot.

The next evening, Carol called me; she was sobbing and could barely talk. She said the doctor had just left her room and told her the result of the blood work that she got two weeks after the first treatment was normal. She went from having stage-four-cancer numbers to normal in two weeks. Carol said to me that she had gotten a miracle! It was difficult for her to comprehend that she was so blessed, but she kept thanking God over and over again. Her tears were tears of joy.

She met with the doctor to go over her new treatment plan, and he told her that she had miraculous results and that he had no words to describe her healing. They removed all the previous drugs and decided to do twenty-minute maintenance treatments. She did three treatments and then stopped them as her CA was now 8. Her follow-up scan revealed that her grapefruit-sized tumor was now the size of a blueberry and not even an issue as they felt it was no longer cancerous. The spleen was clear. The three tumors that were in her liver became calcified and were no longer cancerous. Carol's strong faith and positive attitude and the healing power of prayer resulted in her miraculous healing, and now she had medical proof that it was true.

She has a message that she wants to share with all of us, and it is the message that she shares when she gives her testimony. She says that this story isn't about her but about Jesus Christ. She says that she is not better than anyone else and that Jesus loves us all the same. She is not sharing her story because she is some kind of a hero. She says that Jesus is our hero—the one who gave his life for all of us on the cross. He will heal our worries, our illnesses, and our broken hearts.

Carol said, "We as women worry about our weights and our thighs, but we forget about our souls. And I am not talking about shoes. Jesus will fill our emptiness. He is waiting with open arms. I did not make my CA 125 number tumble. Jesus did. I did not make the doctor say, 'This is miraculous.' Jesus did.

"I did not cause an allergic reaction to the drug to find a blood clot in my lung. Jesus did. I did not make the tumors go away. Jesus did. Jesus wants us to open our hearts and to invite him in. You will never regret that decision. Jesus is accepting applications today. He accepted mine, and he will accept yours."

That is Carol's testimony, and it is not every day that you get to witness a miracle firsthand. I am so blessed to have had the honor and privilege to walk this journey with my friend. The story is not over. It is just beginning. Carol shares her story every time she can to lead others to Jesus Christ. You too have a story to share. It may not seem much to you, but God gives each of us a story to share so we can reach out to others in their times of trouble and give them hope. We do not go through trials and situations in our lives to keep them secret. God will use each of us, and he will give us all that we need to work for him. He is waiting for you to apply for the job that he has already designed for you.

Remember, he created you and has a plan for you, but you have to ask him to use you. And when you do, be prepared to do things that you never imagined were possible! Let go of any anger and unforgiveness that you are holding on to in your heart and receive the love and blessings that God has for you. As Carol said, when you open your heart to him and invite him in, this will become a decision you will never regret. He is waiting on you to call out to him. I pray that you do so today.

I PRAY THAT YOU DO SO TODAY.

LEAVE YOUR FEAR ON THE MOUNTAINSIDE

Jeff Bradley

When a child is brought up with fear, doubt and a false knowledge of God, she knows now the loveliness of Him.

"There is no other," the angel said, and light sprang forth and filled the valley. Who once was a little child was here again.

"Speak softly," she said, "as though I will be made to hear."

Secretly listening, the writer hears all that she says and then remembers.

She played the songs for him once—the ones about a sleepy blue ocean and sunshine so lovely and a whisper of hope resonating in this cloud of fear.

Memories collide—a kind of dream—her bright brown eyes. The smile—a million tears to trade.

"I will not give up," I said, my heart beating.

All the ones she made so beautiful, they still shine, and all the doubts and fears crumble as they speak the words that fell from the angel's lips—like gold dust to fill the mouths.

Not so fast—she would not be taken.

The sun continued to rise beyond the mountain, sunshine falling on the ocean and the silent shore.

"Turn to face the valley and don't look back," the angel said.

The child cried, not knowing God's kindness, and shook her fist at the air.

Above all, in the silence, she did not see God quietly watching, waiting—waiting for her to give this all to him.

The whispers continued. Everything to its season. How much longer?

The child would become a bride. The bride would become a mother and would not fade to gray; she'd been asleep awhile now.

Violets—purple and yellow ones—she showed to me in the spring and brightened the days, and these would continue on—not to be forgotten.

But here, again, a chance to listen.

All the lies and make-believe and all the things that gave life worth were all right in front of her.

"Will you go? Will you come with me?" The watcher waited in silence, still.

And the writer looked down into the valley and at all the dandelions of spring—the seeds scattered across the field by a wind; it was impossible to know where it came from or where it would finally go.

The seeds drifted and danced in the morning light.

God looked down to see if she would accept and then kindly spoke, "My light, my love, my angel, it was finished long ago."

The seeds scattered and ran about with the wind.

"There is a way if you will follow and let these go. Leave your fear on this mountainside, and the doubts will then gather in the coming spring rains and wash into the ravines and then rest at last in the empty ocean. At last, the winter is past, and the springtime has come again. *Arise. Come, my darling, my beautiful one. Come with me.*"

AN EMBRACE OF LOVE

While sorting through items in my jewelry box, I noticed a tiny gold cross that had inadvertently been bent. The arm on each side was bent forward as if to wrap that part of the cross around to the other side. It looked like an embrace—a hug—and I thought of how that was like the *real cross* upon which Jesus died, for Jesus's arms *were* opened wide, and in reality, there *was* an embrace for each one of us on that Calvary cross.

Down through the ages, each one of us can come to that cross and receive our embrace—our hug—our redemption and salvation.

The embrace remains for the lost, for the sinner, for you, for me, and for the whole world. It is a simple prayer that saves, redeems, and makes us whole.

We are redeemed by the spotless Son of God. We are made whole through his sacrifice—a sacrifice of love for us all. We are freed from ourselves, from our sins, and from our despair through the salvation that comes from the cross.

Jesus's love remains—always and forever. His embrace *is* there, waiting for each one of us to say these words that will set us free.

"Lord Jesus, I am sorry for my sins. I repent of them, Lord, and do receive you as the lord and savior of my life. Come into my heart and stay forever!"

And then, we are embraced, we are set free, and we are loved—forever!

THERE IS A LIGHT

Sharon Ann Steele

Death lives. It is alive.

Shielded by walls of self-doubt, regret, worthlessness, and self-hate.

Oh yes, death lives.

It breathes and does its dance—the dance of darkness and condemnation,

Sending jolts of sadness to my soul's core.

Feels like I can't fight this hidden foe.

It's made its home here within,

Infused its very self
Into the walls of my soul.

Yet, there is a light,
A blazing sword,
Protector, defender,
Slicing its foe, settling upon my soul.
His wisdom lights the truth.
My self-pity must flee.
It belongs to the darkness.
I must let it go,
Release it,
Hands free,
To praise God,
And face reality.
My daughter has passed.

WHERE THE TREETOPS GLISTEN

Michael Majoris

During Christmas, the sounds of the season are as much a part of one's experience as all the visual spectacles. With caroling, sleigh bells, children playing, and of course, Santa's laugh, there is a great energy in the air. Folks are more talkative, often beginning conversations about the potential for snow on Christmas or inquiring about the level of shopping completed. I usually just nod or agree during most of the dialogue, but a recent Christmas card that I received resonated deep in me, shaking and stirring my thoughts into a whole new flurry.

I read the handwritten text out loud and then silently a few times.

The greeting was from an older widowed gentleman—a family friend. He wrote of his longing for his wife, now deceased for several years; his need to have to work part-time; and his own personal struggle with a major medical issue. Yet, he still took the time to express himself and wish my family a blessed holiday. I was utterly dumbfounded. There I was, healthy and thriving each day, but I moved through these past few weeks in a regimented way. Preparing for Christmas had turned more into a chore—with dutiful tasks often replacing rejoicing and thankfulness. I looked again at the column of cards decorating our kitchen door. Yes, they were colorful and festive to the eye, and each had a simple nice sentiment, but there was this one card that was essentially crying and reaching out. From these lines of cards to the lines of people shopping, filtering out of church, gathering at school functions, or congregating at work lunch parties, is there more meaningful dialogue that is being spoken? What had I done myself? Had I taken the time to listen?

I decided to at least try to be extra attentive throughout my daily routine. Almost instantly I found that there was always more to the conversation—perhaps not directly stated but still communicated through an inflection in one's voice or sometimes a few stark words like *depressed* or *frustrated*.

While hearing my coworkers interact, I recalled that several of them were spending their first Christmas without a parent or sibling who passed away that year. At my children's after-school activities, I sympathized with regular acquaintances who also felt like there was too much to do while we were trying to figure out what to give everyone as gifts.

Most of the time, however, I was at a loss for words. I listened as a friend spoke of how her husband was fighting depression and how it was very probable that she would not get her Christmas tree up and decorated for her two young daughters. I sat quietly in our living room next to my wife as she conversed on her phone, trying to uplift both her aunt and uncle, who had just recently divorced. During my daily chats with my dad, I heard great worry in his voice as he kept dismissing his scheduled medical test in January. While talking with my sister, I sensed a profound loneliness as she talked about her two college-aged daughters, who were starting to build lives of their own, and how she longed for the bond that we had with our mother; it was now our sixteenth Christmas without her.

For me personally, recently moving away from my dad, sister, and lifelong friends, I felt I lost not only frequent companionship but also a sense of myself and who I am. With my marriage, I would not be honest if I said my wife and I were ending the year with a stronger relationship than how we started the year. Did I really listen to her needs, or did I even try to foster a discussion outside of bills, money, house projects, school, and what the kids required? Why did most of our lengthy conversations only seem to be initiated when we were on edge or in a frenzied state about something? How could we continue to grow together?

As brilliant as Christmas lights are and alongside the festive cheer, there are real cries of anxiety, loss, regret, hurt, fear, and loneliness inside all of us and many unanswered questions. It is no wonder why people often just skim the surface and talk about the weather, but I believe hope still resides in us all—even if it cannot be properly articulated. We all desire a Christmas of white.

Irving Berlin's "White Christmas" has this line: "Just like the ones we used to know." We enjoy seeing the newly fallen snow because it somehow connects us to simpler times in our lives, bringing back a dusting from the landscape of our youth. The perfect sheath of white seems to restore us for the days ahead, temporarily covering up our flawed present selves and offering new chances and opportunities. Additionally, the beautiful frosted pine trees are a sight to behold, but perhaps they also offer us something deeper—a short respite from a hectic day and the means to trade the multitude for a little solitude.

Yes, the "treetops glisten," but as the snowflakes make their way down through the branches, a very faint and soothing rustling can be heard. To describe it is nearly impossible, but its presence is undeniable. It is the sound of our dreams and sorrows and the words that we want to say but cannot express. It is our innermost hopes and prayers and a song that we only hold in our hearts. Alone, we may feel, but it is Jesus among us, helping us embrace it all—the good, the bad, the past, and the present.

"The Lord, your God, is in your midst, a mighty Savior. He will rejoice over you with gladness, and renew you in His love" (Zeph. 3:17, NABRE).

After a few days, one evening, I watched my seven-year-old daughter add her touch of color to a Christmas piece of art, and I asked her, "What does Christmas mean to you?" She simply said, "Love." Maybe that is all we can ever really do—love and give love, take time to be silent in prayer, listen to the falling snow, and try to listen to one another.

A LETTER TO LAURA

When my daughter was a young girl, she was despondent over something and feeling sad. I wrote this little poem to cheer her up.

"Dear Laura,

When we're overwhelmed and blue,

There are some things we can do.

Look for the sun in little places, Like an ice-cream cone,

Or friendly faces.

A patch of blue in a summer sky,

And watching the clouds all roll by,

A square of grass to sit and think,

And ice-cold lemonade to drink,

Flowers that come in different hues,

And hugs and kisses to chase away the blues.

God's smiling face, a hand held out for you,

And all your love will see you through!"

THE TRAGEDY OF TODAY

Still and quiet in his mother's womb,
He lies, unafraid.
He is safe in his huddled nest.
There is no fear in his mother's womb.
His arms are wrapped around his heart.
His legs are bent in comfort.
Muffled sounds enter his domain,
That lull him to sleep.
But then, a tragic happening—
An instrument, sharp and stinging,
Enters his domain.
Something is wrong!
The cord is cut!
A method is used,
And he is robbed of his life.
Still and quiet in his mother's womb,
But he is no longer there,
And God asks, "*Why?*"

SHARING WITH FATHER PETER

Barbara Hervey

In our Bible study, Father Peter encouraged us to reach out to people in need and to pray for them as we witnessed about the love of God for us all.

I was sitting at the downtown bus station, minding my own business and just wanting to get home after a long day at work. Along came an inebriated man. While I was not paying much attention, the person sitting next to me got up, and he sat down. He was in my face when he began speaking to me. He said, "I don't know you."

I responded with "I don't know you."

He then said, "I know you in my conscience. I see what is in your heart."

He laughed, he sang, and he made some inappropriate comments. I was thinking to myself, *What have I gotten into?*

Just six weeks ago, I would have gotten up and found another seat that was far from him.

Instead, I asked him, "Do you pray?"

He said, "Pray? Need to pray in my room." I told him, "We can pray here."

I took out my notebook, which has Scripture verses. I began to read aloud, and he kind of listened to me.

He said, "I can't hear you. The busses are noisy."

I waited until the bus closest to us left and then continued speaking with him and choosing Scripture verses.

I told him, "You are a child of God, and God loves you. You need to believe that Jesus died for your sins and rose again."

He listened to me. The half-empty bottle fell out of his back pocket.

He tucked it back into his pocket.

I saw my bus coming. "What bus are you catching?" I asked. He did not know; he probably had no bus at all.

My bus came. I left, and he just sat there.

On the way home, I thought, *What was I thinking? Did I do okay?* The next morning at work, I found myself thinking about what had happened the day before. I wondered if the man had gotten anything out of the words of Scripture that I spoke. Would he find the strength to overcome his addiction? Did he at least understand that Jesus loves him, no matter what?

Thank you, Father Peter. I am taking tiny steps. I will eventually know what the Lord wants me to do with the rest of my life.

Thank you for listening.

A BUNNY

Did God *touch* you before you became a bunny so cute before my eyes?

You dared not look at me directly

But gave me a sideward glance, looking at me while not moving your head,

Watching while deciding what you should do.

I stood there, watching also, as you gently hopped to the next patch of grass,

Looking for sweet clover in your midst.

Do you know?

A bunny fresh from the *Creator's hand*—

You spread magic wherever you go,

For you came

From the Creator's heart—

A touch of magic

For earth below!

GRIEF

Father, help me deal with the grief in my heart.

I am lonely. I am hurting. I need help.

The grief tears me apart.

Oh, put me back together again.

I kneel at your feet.

I am sorry for anything that is not love in my heart.

Erase the bitterness; erase the scar.

The scar needs to be changed—changed into love.

We are here only for a short time.

Our real home is heaven.

Help me embrace love here, and love will erase all wounds.

We *are* together in love—my loved one and I.

We will always be together in love—for all of eternity.

Thank you, Father, for love.

Amen.

THE OUR FATHER

Our Father—my Father, my God,

Who art in heaven—in your place of glory, of majesty—in your honor,

Hallowed be *thy* name—forever and ever and ever!

Thy kingdom come. May it come now, Father.

Thy will be done—all over the earth—in all of us—in all peoples everywhere,

On earth as it is in heaven—just as it is in heaven.

Give us this day our daily bread. We ask for all our needs,

And forgive us our trespasses. We are sorry for all that we have done wrong,

As we forgive those who have trespassed against us. We forgive all, Father, just as you

Have forgiven us!

And lead us not into temptation. Help us surmount all our temptations,

But deliver us from evil. Deliver us from all the wiles of the devil and evil.

Amen! So be it, Father! So be it!

PART 2

"THUS, WILL I BLESS YOU ALL OF MY DAYS. LIFTING UP MY HANDS I WILL CALL UPON YOUR NAME.

AS WITH THE RICHES OF A BANQUET SHALL MY SOUL BE SATISFIED, AND WITH EXULTANT LIPS, MY MOUTH SHALL GIVE YOU PRAISE."

SEARCHING

As wise men of old looked for a star,
I look for mine.
Is life so cold and bleak
That no star shines?
I wait. I wonder. I look.
I see a heart filled with love,
With caring.

I see a star.

I see wounds healed by kindness,

By compassion.

I see a star.

I wait. I wonder,

Can it be?

Is *love* the answer?

I reach out to one cold and unfriendly.

I blanket them with love,

And now,

I find the star!

GRANDPA, SALAMANDERS, AND THE RIVER-STREAM WIDE

Jeff Bradley

He walks down the hill fast—into the river-stream wide. This afternoon is warm—too warm for September. The sycamores bend their leaves upward to curl around the sun. September rolls on, and great roots stretch deep to drink. The water swirls around him now as he wades into the stream—a curl of foam rises from the ripples behind him—and the water up ahead shoots backward in an ever-circling arc. Will it ever change if it never rains again? The stream always had its magic. These seeds were planted long ago.

He pauses now, pondering and disturbing this stillness—the stillness that is ever perfect without his presence there. He wonders where he fits into all of this. He wades deeper, navigating around a larger rock, the water encompassing him always no matter where his next step lands. He remembers a waterfall that he once saw long ago. Time, distance, and memories collide, and he arrives, after a brief moment, lost back here. With a cast into the eddy, the lure flies. He drops it lightly as to somehow belong here now that he has the time to think. A tick of the line transferred complete, and a smallmouth bass rockets skyward. Sunlight gleams on bronze, and he wonders how he is allowed to play this part so profound. Bronze, gold, and those orange-brown eyes—eyes that the sun always makes more beautiful. It was a cast of fate that is now held close. He feels the passage of something circular, and for a moment, he feels a part of the fish's life. His hand reaches out to return it back home. He smiles, as always, and sighs.

Where to begin? He thinks about a spring creek when he was a little boy, catching minnows and salamanders. The water was dark and surrounding him. He could smell the cool earth and see green everywhere. The water had bathed him then, and he was baptized by its constancy, flowing around and around. It had changed him then, hadn't it? Certainly he was never the same afterward.

Just like the stream here—the water moving as the colors change with the light.

September colors were different, dry colors, the end of summer— sycamores yellow and brown and the bark that soon would almost glow in the dark. The sugar maples were now dyed yellow and orange— colors that this river would surely wash away in the end. It had done as much before. The days were growing shorter.

Up around the bend, he hears the sounds of an end-of-summer gathering—grand but mournful.

The echoed voices stretch, bounding into the afternoon. He lifts his head to listen, and after hearing them, he realizes. The water is still. Up ahead, the bridge lies across the stream, formed by more great sycamores, and the mountain, looming straight up, is almost purple in the slanted light.

The road is still as a dark-gray silhouette, and the bridge pier is jet-black, shooting up from the water below. The water had once been quite deep—they used to jump here—but now, the piling sat partially on dry land, surrounded by a sea of river rock and brown-gray weeds. September had taken its toll. The handrail on the bridge appeared as a gossamer ribbon in the distant haze. It curved with the road below, its tapestry caught in the blue hue of the mountains bending low enough to reach it.

The water was quite clear in this stream. It shimmered like crystal where it met rocks that were not completely submerged. The pools ahead, however, were dark and still—at least at the surface. This green-black color probably existed nowhere else in the world, but then again, he thought, that old Johnson fishing reel was as such.

He saw his grandfather's hands wrapped around it, reeling. It had rained that day, he remembered. Bass and salamanders. Bass and salamanders. He had thought it sad—on the part of the salamanders, at least—and had secretly set one free—a special one, for sure. Its eyes were dark, but they seemed to regard the young boy. The eyes—wet like polished glass—looked out. And so it was stolen away from the white bucket and released so that it could face its own fate. He watched it swim away.

The evening came on, and they would drive home together. He kept looking up at the side of his grandpa's face while realizing what had been given to him. The days would pass, and he would think of the salamander now and again. He would remember his dark eyes, and sometimes, when he was alone, he would cry, not really knowing why.

OH, LORD

Oh, Lord, how plenteous are your ways in all the world.

Oh, Lord, you are the maker, and your works are *good* over all the earth.

We see your fingerprints forming, shaping, and giving to *all*.

The mountains were but a breath from your mouth,

The hills and distant valleys just a word from your lips.

Your hands fashioned man from dust and Eve from a rib,

And all the cosmos, in a colorful array,

Did spin and twirl and show their thankfulness to you.

And I, a poor creature here,

So hollow and so filled with

My own designs,

Can break off the yoke that sets me bound

To me and mine

And look to you.

To raise a hand to you in praise,

To let my mouth sing praises rare,

And to let my eyes soar up to you.

To seek your face,

To hear your words,

And to be fulfilled in you

And to give you your rightful due.

I am not the Creator. I am not.

I, lowly though I be,

Can still sing to you

And speak my praise to you.

Oh, Holy One, I do not deserve your glance,

But love does fill your heart

For all that live.

And I, as one living now,

Do extend my heart, my love,

My hand to you

To keep me safe

For all eternity.

Amen!

AN OPEN LETTER TO SOMEONE CONTEMPLATING SUICIDE

Dear Desperate Soul,

My heart aches for you, your anguish and pain, and your total disillusionment with life. *Life* is a *precious* gift that we often take for granted—*all* of us. We live our lives in a frenzy and take little rest. We have relationships that don't work. We get involved with things that are harmful to our bodies and our souls, and then we blame *life* for our unhappiness.

The meaning of life is so much more. Our lives are *not* our own. This is the first key to understanding life as it really is. *Life* is a *gift*. We are *not our own*. We belong to God, and he has seen fit to have placed us here—in this time and place—for a reason.

Each of us has a *job* to do here—a work that God ordained for *each* one of us. Our earthly life is only a stopover on our journey to the greater life of eternity. The *greatest mistake* we can do is miss out on this opportunity to do the *work* that we were meant to do.

If life dealt hard blows to you—in rejection, in heartache, in pain, in suffering, and in disappointment and death—know that these are parts of our earthly life that we cannot escape. *All* of us must deal with these things at one point or another.

There is no perfect life on this earth. We build our lives with the "blocks" of all the happenings of our lives and hopefully build not a dungeon but a temple. We *offer* to God *all these happenings*, and they are transformed into something that *can* bring good to ourselves and others by our willingness to let go of any negative emotions, such as fear, anger, worry, self-pity, doubt, and despair.

We are *all* rejected and torn. We all have bruises in our hearts. But to those who can *endure* these things and *rise above them* with a life of service for others, the *prize* belongs to them.

If we are waiting for happiness to mysteriously come to us by itself, it does not happen. But if we choose to *give*, to *enjoy*, and to *bless* others by an act, a word, or a thought of ours, happiness comes to them *and* to us.

The Lord, in his mysterious way, has chosen *you* to be here *now* to do the *work* that will also make *you* happy.

Within you, you have the power to surmount any difficulty and make

your life a shining example of faith, hope, and trust in life itself and in God, who gives life to us all.

I pray that the darkness will leave you and that the light will come into your life now and stay forever!

God bless you and keep you in his care always and forever.

Carolyn

MY ANGEL

Oh, angel at my side,

I have not given you a sideward glance.

So many days we have been together here on earth.

I have not thought of all that you do—

All that you can and always do.

So within my heart this day,

I say to you,

"I love you, holy angel.

Stay by my side

Always

And guide and guard me

And lead me to heaven

Someday!"

GOD AND THE APPLE TREE

Years ago, a little girl fell from an apple tree. She was a beautiful little girl—so kind, so tender, and so loving. She had been saying her prayers in that tree in our side yard. She had climbed the tree as a little seven-year-old to be "closer to God" while she prayed.

Suddenly, she had fallen. She had fallen onto the hard ground, scraping her arms and legs, and came into our house, crying and bewildered. She had gotten hurt superficially, but her real hurt was deep within.

"Why did God allow me to fall?" She told me words of pain and disbelief. Her heart was deeply wounded, and her eyes showed disappointment, sadness, and a deep questioning of the ways of God.

I tried to explain to her that God doesn't cause hurt or disappointment or pain and that God is here with us to help us *through* the pain and heartaches, as a good father does. The earth will have its trials. We will all have our times of sorrow and pain. We will all have our own "apple trees," but God's promise to us is that he will never leave us or forsake us.

I comforted her that day in the best way that I could. I cleaned and bandaged her wounds, but I knew that the real bandage needed to be around her heart.

The little girl grew up to be a wonderful young lady—caring, sharing, and giving—with a strong faith in the love and presence of God. The apple tree still stands in our yard—a sign of questioning, trust, and reaching. Reach up to the Creator—to our Father—who promises to be with us always and forever. *And he is!*

WORRY

Josie Pate

A dark cloud over my head,
A black hole,
A knot in my stomach.

Fear of the unknown?
Not able to "measure up"?
Deal with?
Do the right thing?
"And all will be well."

"Look at the birds."
"Consider the lilies."
"Are you not of more value?"
"Can worrying add a
Single hour to Your life?"

Trust! Amen!

FATHER

What does it mean to call you, Father? What does it mean to see your love, your kindness, and your joy when you think of me? I never knew you as Father for so long. I didn't know, but now I do. You are love for me—for everyone. You hear our prayers, and you answer them in love and respect. I give you my heart now and forever. I will always love you. *Thank you for all that you have done for me in my life.* I wish to praise you and honor you and adore you forever! I wish to give you all that I have. I wish to serve *you* forever! Amen.

THE ART OF THANKSGIVING

We teach our children and grandchildren when they are little to say "Thank you" when they are given a gift or receive a favor. Perhaps *we* need someone to remind us over and over again to say "Thank you" to God.

When we are grateful, we are happy. God wants us to have happy hearts full of thanksgiving, knowing that this will help us see life more clearly and truthfully. Teaching children to be grateful expands their hearts so that they see the wonder of life and the wonder of giving and receiving. Teaching *us* to be grateful does the same.

Thanksgiving is the key to productive work and a happy heart. We are all children of God, and learning to say "Thank you" is for our own benefit as well as others.

God knows that being grateful fills our hearts with hope and joy. When we do encounter difficulties in our lives, we can still look for a reason for thanksgiving and to be grateful for the blessings that we *do* have already.

We need to break through the clouds of worry, doubt, fear, and mistrust by doing a simple act of faith and trust in God: Saying "Thank you" to him for his presence, help, and care in all our concerns and heartaches.

Thanksgiving is a blessing for us that enables us to *see* things differently and opens the door to peace, contentment, and trust.

Thank you, God, for all! Amen.

A HAPPY THOUGHT

"Whatsoever things are lovely, pure, noble, of good report . . . think on those things, and the God of Peace will be with us" (Phil. 4:8–9).

What we *think* determines *how we feel,* and we need to give our minds a break from the anxieties, the doubts, and the fears that plague us all. We need to *train our minds* to think on those things that will *give* our minds rest, peace, and a sense of well-being.

We need to substitute a *worrisome* thought for a *blessed* thought—a happy thought. We *can* find a blessing during our journeys. We can look through a situation and still find something to hold on to. We can understand that life takes many turns. This is not the end. *There will be help, hope, and love from God always!*

There is a way to find God's help in all: We must use our willingness to set aside doubt, fear, and worry and take one step and then another while knowing that God sees, God knows, and God will *never* fail to help.

We *always* have help available in God, and that is the secret to happy thoughts and a happy way for us all!

A CAROLINA WREN

There was a Carolina wren who loved to sit on the railing of our deck and sing her song. It was a very definite, clear sound—one that caught your attention.

I marveled, while going through an illness that I had, that she would perch on the railing and sing as if from her heart, cheering up the surroundings.

I had a number of issues to deal with, and each time, as my heart grew saddened, I would hear her tune and be uplifted and strengthened by her song.

Each time I grew saddened, I would hear the notes, which were crystal clear, and I would look for her, and there she would be, all alone and singing her song. I was uplifted and comforted so many times that I began to think that perhaps an angel was sending her to me.

My illness got better, but her song stays with me in my heart—a part of God's creation that brings comfort, hope, and strength to me.

Thank you, Carolina wren. Thank you, God!

My mother, Ann, passed away at the age of 100 in April of last year. It was close to Mother's Day, and I remembered how we celebrated so many wonderful Mother's Days with her. She is a model for all mothers with her hardworking care of her children—always giving her love, help, and support and always making things seem better because she was there. She was full of wisdom and God's grace and helped us whenever we needed help, advice, or someone to talk to. This is a poem that I wrote for her.

HER FIRST MOTHER'S DAY IN HEAVEN

Her first Mother's Day in heaven,
She is beside the Lord so dear.
She breathed her last but shed no tear,
For her purpose was so clear.

She had to pass through the veil,
That separates the earth and sky,
And then, as God would have it,
The angels taught her how to fly.

She flew with golden wings to God,
Within the angel's arms,
And heaven's gates opened wide,
And there was no alarm.

For there stood Jesus, smiling there,
And she on bended knee,
And words of welcome came from his lips,
No happier than could she be.

"Welcome, child. You've come so far.
You've done all that you should.
You've done your duty, giving Mother's love,
And lived your life the best that you could.

Mother's roses are all round
You this Mother's Day,
For you have given your children
The safest place to stay."

Within the Savior's arms, you told them
The story of his life,
How Jesus came to be our Savior
And to battle all our strife.

For everything lies in Jesus's arms,
And he gives all the right

To conquer sin and troubles and sorrows
By being in his light.

For his light is love and hope and strength.
He gives us joys abounding.
For in his heart is all the cure
For all the cares we're sounding.

And mothers have a special place
Because of the children they do grow,
Up in kindness, love, and hope,
And Jesus's heaven's rewards do bestow.

"And so, Ann, you see your children down below.
It all is worth the living,
For a task of love is greater than a gift,
And your heart keeps on the giving."

So *Happy Mother's Day, dear Mom!*
We send you our hearts and our love.
To the *best mother ever*,
Now with Jesus in heaven above!

A TIME TO HOPE

Hoping takes time and patience. Hope is feeling that help or strength or joy will come in the end. There is always a reason to hope, for there is always a reason to love—to love God, who is all hope, who can do all, and who is able and willing to help in all situations.

If we could see God the way that he really is, we would never doubt! Jesus knew the Father. He said, "I and the Father are One."

They are one in love, in caring, and in service. Jesus said, "When you see me, you see the Father."

What was Jesus like? He showed us his love. He went to the cross while knowing the anguish that he was going to endure—the pain, the torment, and the untold agony that he would suffer for me, for you, and for all of humanity so that we would be saved from our sins. Jesus's way was to love beyond measure—to give of himself, his help, his healing, and his service to all.

God is a loving God, a serving God, and a prayerful God. He loves to *hear* our prayers. He loves to respond in depth to our prayers. He does not turn a deaf ear to our pleadings, to our needs, and to our intentions. He greatly grants all that can be given to us and to all of humanity.

We serve a serving God, and that is why there is always a reason to hope, to love, to care, and to serve others. We learn from *our* serving God, who loves to serve. We serve as he does with his heart, with his mind, and with his arms, which are given to us in love forever. We serve a mighty God, and *that* is our hope and our reason to hope forever!

PRAISE

When we are distraught and feeling low,
Praise is the only way to go.
Praise brings the sunshine to sparkle the day,
For we know that help is on the way.
So lift your voice in beauteous praise
To the loving God, who knows all our ways.
He will bring sunshine as soon as he can,
For we know that is in his holy plan.
So start to sing whether you feel like it or not
And say, "Oh, Lord, *your* work with wonders are wrought!"
For there isn't a dark cloud that he can't change to white,
For he alone is the King of Light.
So light *will* come, and your heart will *know*,
That your bounteous praise made it so!

A TIME TO SHARE

Sharing takes time and patience and caring.

When we share, we give away a part of ourselves, our possessions, our caring, or our love.

We share because we believe there is a higher calling in life, a higher purpose, a call to do extraordinary actions through very ordinary ways.

"To give a cup of water to the thirsty," Jesus said, "will be rewarded at the end of time with a Kingdom—a Kingdom of Love."

It is a privilege to share; it is a blessing for ourselves and others, and it is a way of life— a humble way, a serving way, and a purposeful way.

We give as we are given but even more.

We give as we have not to give of our needy plight, to make an even greater sacrifice, because we do not have "plenty." The widow with the two coins gave all she *could* have been able to give,

But she gave—gave with a generous heart.

"And this woman has put in more than all of the others." Sometimes we give, even in our need,

To open a door—a door that releases blessings to ourselves and to others.

We give as we are given while not counting the cost, for Jesus is

Lord.

He gave *all*—his time, his talents, his treasures—to *everyone*!

As the throngs of humanity clamor for their needs of warmth, food, and happiness,

We can do *our* part—even in our own need.

We *can* bless with two small coins given in love— given as the opportunities arise,

Looking for these opportunities with a kind and loving heart.

Each of us has two coins.

May we give them

In love! Amen!

JOY'S GIFT

Joy is God's way of saying "I love you" to each of us. Joy comes from the heart of God and springs into our own hearts by our willingness to trust, believe, and hope in a merciful, kind, loving, and benevolent God. Joy is a gift from God's heart and flows into our own hearts as we empty our own hearts of all that is destructive to joy. Joy has to have calmness and rest of spirit. Joy cannot dwell in chaos, in unrest, and in self-seeking. The secret to joy is a docile and peaceful spirit—a spirit that takes God at his word. God's words are truthful.

Jesus said, "Come to Me all you who labor and are heavy laden, and I will give you rest. Take My yoke upon you, and learn from Me, for I am meek and humble of heart and you will find rest for your souls, for my yoke is easy and my burden is light" (Matt. 11:28–30, ESV).

"How can our burdens be light?" we might ask when we feel overwhelmed, tired, weary, and heartsick. Jesus has the answer. The answer is within us. We must first take Jesus's yoke upon us and learn from him who is "meek and humble of heart." A gentle spirit lies still and quiet in God's arms and does not seek on its own but seeks a higher mystery for its life. It is one of looking to God for sustenance, help, grace, and guidance. The will of God is foremost in a meek and humble heart and brings rest and peace and, in the end, joy—true joy. After relinquishing all to God, we find the first stirrings of joy in our souls. As we pray and do our daily tasks, they take on new meanings and brighter hues as we, with open arms, receive this gift moment by moment and fulfill the will of God in our lives.

Father, I receive this gift of joy and ask that I may do your will always. Amen.

A SOUL

Oh, created soul, what great treasure is yours,
That in this time and space,
A life was given to you.
I can run and play and dream.
I can speak and hear and sing
And live a gift of life so sublime
That it was given without any payment from me.
A life freely given, freely blessed, and freely loved
By a creator so divine.
To think in little terms
Such as me—
A tiny soul—
And yet the hand outstretched comes to me
And holds out a hand of love to set me free,
And I can only say *yes*—
Yes to him.
Yes to love.
Yes to peace—forever! Amen.

PERHAPS

Perhaps there is no greater joy on earth
Than to see the child that was carried in the womb.
To see the features, hear the heartbeat,
And touch the limbs so free.

Perhaps there is no greater time on earth
Than that of looking at our child—
To see their face and well-bloomed cheeks
And tiny hands and fingers pearl.

Perhaps there is no greater touch on earth

Than the touch of our child's hand in ours—

To feel the softness of the hand and to know that a greater plan than we fashioned

Each tiny hand with softness and love.

Perhaps there is no greater sound on earth

Than hearing our child speak their words—

Words that echo through the earth

That God is love And God so chose

To share his love with me!

A TIME TO BELIEVE

Believing takes time, patience, and trust. If we trust, we *can* believe. If we reach out to truth, we can believe and have reasons *to believe*. We believe because God is real. He cares and he loves. Sometimes we can't see, we can't hope, or we can't trust, but we know there is still *God*—the Almighty, the Healer, and the *Truth* of All Creation.

No matter what happens, there is still *God*. No matter what we feel, it does not diminish or change or alter the reality and presence of God. He is as real as our breathing—as real as the touch of our fingers upon our faces. He breathes life and *gives* life and shares his life with others—with you, with me, with all.

His is a life that gives and shares and keeps giving. Without God, there would be *nothing*. To try to change, alter, or malign his name is a blasphemy of the highest proportions. To *change God* is to alter *truth*. *Truth* is reality. *Truth* cannot be changed or misrepresented.

What is there to think about God? To think about God is to discover *truth*, and *truth* sets us free. To learn to serve and love God is the essence of our true existence. To live *with him* for all eternity in the blessedness of his kingdom is the goal of all his children.

To *believe* is to allow our hearts to give him his due. God gives *us* his intended gifts, which were given in love for us all!

IF YOU COULD

If you could go back one summer,
Where would you go?
To a field, to a stream,
To an ocean's wave on the blue?

If you could *capture* one moment
From a distant past
And set it upon your heart—
So good and true—

If you could taste one savory delight again
From the house wherein you lodged
And smell the sweet aroma
All through and through.

If you could bring back one smile
From someone's lips
That cheered your heart,
Then please do—

For memories live but for the pleasure of those

Who have spent their years on earth,

And all that was good beautifies the earth

In whatever we savor and do.

So that in some far-off clime of heaven's joys and beauty,

There rises from the earth those sweet memories that are good and true,

And these sweet memories make the earth

A better place for me and you.

A TIME FOR FORGIVENESS

We need to forgive ourselves, others, and the circumstances that may have caused us to be hurt. We need to forgive because it is healing for *ourselves* when we do forgive.

To forgive is to allow the mercy, patience, trust, and love of God to permeate *our* beings, and then we can bestow this on others—

> On those who have wounded us,
>
> On those who have severed ties with us,
>
> On those who have estranged themselves from us.
>
> Forgiveness is a blessing that enriches all of us—
> body, mind, and soul.
>
> *Let us forgive!*

COVER THE EARTH

Come, Holy Spirit. Enlighten the darkness.
Let thy healing rays cover the earth
With softness and light.

Come, Holy Spirit. Enlighten each heart.
Send healing, send truth, send peace.
Cover the earth with warmth—
All by God's might.

Come, Holy Spirit. You are one with the Father, one with the Son.
Look in each corner of the earth—from sea to sea.
Look, Holy Spirit.
Make all things right!

PACKING OUR BAGS

When my grandson, Corey, had to ride along with my husband and me to take me to work, he found the ride very tedious. I noticed him one day "packing his bag." He took a paper bag and filled it with a few of his treasured articles. Being five years old at the time, there were a few small cars that he had chosen, a superhero figure, tiny toy soldiers, a small bag of cookies, and a large green dinosaur that had peeped over the top of the bag. Corey was ready for anything and prepared to enjoy the ride.

Sometimes during life's lessons and journeys, we may need to "pack our bags" so that we can be ready for anything that may come our way and find comfort, hope, and joy in our daily happenings.

For our moments of discouragement, we need to bring along the virtues of hope and trust while keeping in mind these words:

"Blessed be the Lord, who daily loads us with benefits" (Ps. 68:19, NKJV).

In moments of fear and darkness, we can rely on the light and love of God to give us safety and security.

"God is light and in Him is no darkness at all" (1 John 1:5, NKJV). "The Lord is my light and my salvation, whom shall I fear?" (Ps.

27:1, NKJV).

In temptation and weariness, we can call on God's blessed Son to give us the strength to overcome all obstacles.

"Blessed is the man who endures temptation, for when he has been approved, he will receive the crown of life which the Lord has promised to those who love Him" (Ja. 1:12, NKJV).

In our times of sickness and pain, we can feel the cooling hand of the Savior, who himself "has born our griefs and carried our sorrows" (Isa. 53:4, NKJV) and "He himself took our infirmities and bore our sicknesses" (Matt. 8:17, NKJV).

At our final moments of facing death and dying, we need to see a new life—a risen life—and hold the hand of the risen Savior.

"Yea, though I walk through the valley of the shadow of death, I will fear no evil, for You are with me, YOUR rod and YOUR staff they comfort me" (Ps. 23:4, NKJV).

Life's lessons *can* be learned in many ways, and a rainbow of happiness is within reach of us all, for love can be found everywhere in happy hearts and happy faces as we find blessings in our own lives to share with others.

The important thing that we must remember is that we should not allow "our bags" to be packed with negative emotions and feelings. We must rid ourselves of these immediately so that the full joy and exuberance for life can go along with us wherever we go.

Corey's bag held all the things that he needed for his trip. If we take along faith, hope, trust, love, and joy, we too will have all that we will ever need!

AN OBSTRUCTED VIEW

While watching a baseball game in a nearby stadium, I noticed how our previous seats the week before had a much-better view. The seats had been higher, and the view had been spectacular. Down below, only the tops of the edifices were apparent, and the lights were somehow dimmed by the obstructed view.

I thought of how we may need to "climb the heights" in our own lives to get a better view of all of life's situations and happenings. Oftentimes in life, things can obstruct our view or get in the way of reality.

We may think that there is a monster of fear before our eyes when, in reality, there is nothing there, or perhaps the situation doesn't merit the imagined fear. We can look away from the unreality and see *Jesus* in our daily lives. *He* is the reality. *He* is the *better view*.

No matter the situation, pain, disappointment, heartbreak, confusion, anger, and misjudgment, we can turn to *Jesus*, who is above our trials and seemingly hopeless situations.

There is hope for all of us when we accept our trials and hardships while knowing that God cares, that God loves, and that God is with us always.

The view that we see in all is *Jesus*, God's holy Son. We will see clearly. We will be able to bear all. We will know the truth in him—in *Jesus*. All the clouds will disappear, and the view will be *spectacular*!

KINDNESS

Father, teach us to be kind.
Help us live with kindness in our hearts,
With kindness on our lips,
and with kindness in our thoughts.
Let us never react in any unkindness,
no matter what the circumstances.
This will please your heart and bless our own hearts.
Let kindness flow as a holy stream out of our hearts
and into the lives of others.
Let this be a blessing in our lives—
to live every day being kind to ourselves,
to our families, and to all that we meet each day.
Father, give the world the breath
of your kindness through us.
In Jesus's name, we pray.
Amen.

DEPRESSION

My heart is cold, torn. Self-pity grips at my soul.

Depression brings its clawlike fingers, tightening over my heart. My heart cries,

"When will it stop?"

And then, a whispered prayer— "Praise" is the word.

"Father, I praise—I praise you for all— All that has occurred,

All that will be.

I praise."

My heart is a garment of white. Praise lifts the veil of darkness. *Praise*!

BENT TREES

Thank you, Lord, for bent trees that sway in the wind,

showing me that I too must bend.

Thank you, Lord, for the wood of the cross, which teaches me that pain is a part of life—a part we cannot escape,

but pain is a jewel, a hidden jewel, when we accept it and learn from it.

Thank you, Lord, for bent trees

that sway in the wind and do not break.

Help me not to break.

Amen.

THE GIFT OF PEACE

Peace is God's gift to us all. Peace comes when we allow God to *be* God in our lives. When we love God, we can see him as he is—totally loving, caring, and devoted to our well-being. God wants us all to live with peace, to enjoy peace, and to give peace to others.

"Peace I leave with you, My peace I give to you, not as the world gives, do I give it to you" (John 14:27, NKJV).

To accept the gift of peace, all that we have to do is relinquish all to God, placing everything in his hands while knowing that he will do what is best for us and for all. If we are burdened with doubts, fears, sufferings, and trials, we can still find peace by our willingness to look for peace from God.

He can turn doubt into faith, fear into trust, and our sufferings and trials into jewels of great mercy and love. Our sufferings and trials take on new meanings when we place them in God's hands while asking him to be with us and sustain us through them all.

As we do this, life becomes clearer and newer. Life takes on a *new meaning* as we venture forth with God and live life in his presence and relinquish all to him.

Whatever the trial or whatever the suffering, we can *know* that God will never leave us or forsake us. We can *know* that he will be with us each step of the way with his pardon, comfort, strength, and love.

Knowing this gives us the gift of peace.

Father, give us the gift of peace in Jesus's name. Amen.

SAVING

Jesus, take care of us all.
Protect us.
Send us a mighty throng of angels
To heal the land.
Send miracles everywhere.
Send love freely.
Take the seeds of love that are planted
And make them grow all over the world.
Save the children.
Save the adults.
Save, dear Jesus!
Save!

THE ACHE

The ache I feel could fill the ocean; grief, pain, rejection—
steel slicing into my heart—my soul.
Is there a way to bear this?
I kneel down and look up.
There is one—
one who knows pain, rejection—
steel slicing into his heart.
He was there on Calvary. He looked up.
"Father, it is finished. I come." Now I myself come.
I come to feel his comfort.
I allow his arms to hold me up.
I can stand in him—only in him.
He cares for me.
He knows.
Amen.

A SILENT NIGHT

I worked in a nursing home. There was a clamor of noises every day: buzzers ringing, door alarms sounding, room lights beeping, and a myriad of other noises of every kind. Days were hectic and stress-filled due to the pressing orders and tasks. There was little time to "take a breather" and realize what was really going on around us.

On one special day, I was blessed beyond anything I could imagine. I was talking with a resident who had been helped to get ready to go to sleep that night, and I stopped in her room to say "Good night." She was one hundred years old and did not understand where she was but knew that she was not at home. She looked at me with slate-blue eyes and said that it was nice to talk to me.

I noticed on her shelf a white music box with a carved nativity scene displayed around its outer borders. A white glass Christmas tree stood in the center. Even though it was not the Christmas season, I asked her if she would like to hear it play, and she nodded in agreement. I wound up the music box, wondering if it would even play, and suddenly, the room was filled with the sounds of a Christmas carol.

"Silent night, holy night. All is calm, all is bright."

The notes were sweet and clear, and the room took on a different tone—as if all the other clamorous noises were hushed. Only the music box's notes prevailed on the ear. We both listened, and as I looked around the room, I thought of what a sacred moment this was. What seemed to be a hectic, noise-filled workday suddenly became holy, still, and peaceful.

Her eyes showed recognition as she too listened—as though she was taken back to another place and time. She smiled softly as the notes continued, and we both waited for the song to end as it gently soothed our cares away.

Perhaps we *all* need to hear such a tune play in our hearts again and again so that it can revive us and make us new and refreshed. On our darkest days or during pain-filled nights, we need to listen for such a tune to spin the world back to reality again and to know that there is still a silent night and a time of peace for us all.

Our hearts *can* still sing. Our ears *can* still hear melodies in our hearts that we will always remember.

As the resident laid her head back against her pillow, I tucked her covers up around her, squeezed her hand so softly, and said, "*Good night!*"

THE WAY

Jesus, when you said,
"I am the way"—
Show us the way.

When you said,
"I am the truth"—
Give us the truth.

When you said, *"I am the life"*—
Show us the life—
The true *life*—
That only comes from *you.*
Amen.

FAITH

Faith is not so much seeing as believing. Faith is believing in God— in what he can do and what he cannot do. God *can* do everything good. God *cannot* do anything wrong.

We look to God in our lives for help, comfort, and guidance. We also look to God to make us new. God can make each of us new in some way by teaching us to be more loving, more faithful in our daily duties, and more joyful. It takes faith to be joyful.

Life is full of trials, temptations, and hurdles. If we look to God, we can surmount anything that life brings to us. We can believe that God is real, that he is there to help us, and that he knows what we are going through.

We can take God's hand in all our daily difficulties and know that we are not alone.

"Yes, Father, we do take your hand. Give us strength, comfort, peace, and joy in all our difficulties. We know that you will always be with us and will never leave us. Thank you for the gift of faith. Amen."

LOVING LORD

Loving Lord,

You sent Jesus to us to show us how much you truly love each of us. Open our hearts so that we might grow in kindness and helpfulness to others.

Help us to forgive when others hurt us.

Help us to share what we can with those who are in need. Give us smiling hearts and faces to match

So that we may rejoice in the love that Jesus came to share with us.

Amen!

PART 3

"WHY ARE YOU SO DOWNCAST, OH MY SOUL, AND WHY DO YOU SIGH WITHIN ME? HOPE THOU IN GOD, FOR

I SHALL YET PRAISE HIM, MY SAVIOR AND MY GOD."

STARTING FOR HOME

My earliest memories are playing outside in our yard with the swings that my dad had made for us. One had a type of motor at the top of a long metal pole with chains dangling to the swings that would turn the swings in a circle, like the ones in the carnival. Another swing was a four-seater wooden swing, two seats facing each other, with a wooden floor that swung back and forth. What wonderful times with our neighborhood friends!

There were three of us: my older sister, Barbara; my younger brother, Jimmy; and me. Barbara is three years older than me, and Jim is eighteen months younger.

We lived in a little coal-mining town in Western Pennsylvania. We lived in a rented house, a double house, with other occupants on the left part of the house. We had a kitchen, a living room, two bedrooms upstairs, and a sun porch at the back. I would play on the steps with my red-haired baby doll, which I loved, and I loved painting with my watercolors and always asked Santa for a baby doll and art supplies.

We didn't have a lot of money. My father worked in one of the coal mines in our town, but he sometimes didn't work many hours, and one time, he had health issues, having to go to Cleveland Clinic to be examined for an enlarged heart. We stayed with my grandma on my father's side, who also lived in the town. We were happy when the report came back negative, and he was able to work again.

My mother was the heart of our home, always baking, cooking, and sewing our clothes. She even made the habits of the nuns who taught at the Slovak Church parish school, Saints Cyril and Methodius, which was adjacent to the church. My mother was always busy, doing her chores and helping to make our home comfortable and happy. She didn't have extra money to decorate, but she always had our home looking beautiful—even with the used furniture. She would wallpaper and paint other items to match, like the little plaster of paris violins that hung on the wall. She would paint these the color of the wallpaper, put flowers on the kitchen table, and make new curtains and drapes for the living room.

I loved my mother; she was everything to me. She was kind, prayerful, strong, and loving and had such good wisdom. Whatever problems we had, we knew that we could go to my mother, and she always had an answer or a solution or a bit of advice that helped us see it all more clearly.

My mother's mother, Suzanna, was also very kind, prayerful, and loving. My maternal grandfather, George, was kind also, and my mother had a wonderful childhood with such wonderful parents. My mother had two sisters and three brothers, and sadly, she lost a sister, Susan, to pneumonia; Susan was six at the time, and my mother was three. They said my grandmother was never totally the same after losing her daughter. The doctor had come to the house and said there was nothing they could do for her. At that time, there were no antibiotics. Her little grave lies in the church cemetery in the town.

My grandmother had a wonderful carpet loom in the shed in her backyard. I would watch her picking out the pieces of cloth and then putting them through the loom. I marveled at the beautiful rugs that she made, each one different, and she gave them as gifts or used them on her own kitchen floor. We always had some in our kitchen—sturdy, useful, and beautiful.

My grandfather was a quiet man but had much love in his heart for everyone, especially for my grandmother. She was ill with diabetes at an early age, and he always tried to help her with the chores of the day. My mother told me that he would get up during the night when my mother had an earache, and he would put the soothing oil in her ear. My mother was the second to the youngest in her family, so her older brothers were very attentive to her and her two sisters.

One of the chores that my own mother had during the day was to take their geese to the creek below their house and let them get water, feed them, and watch them for a time. Her friend Tillie joined her, and they played card games and other games. My mother didn't mind being the "Goose Girl" at all as she had her own fun during the times she had to stay with them. My grandma baked fresh bread every day, and she would give large slices of it—with butter and jelly—to my mom and her friends.

My dad started dating my mother when she was eighteen years old; she was still in high school. He was older than her, nine years older, and her mom had her concerns about her dating someone so much older.

She was enthralled by his handsome looks, dark hair, brown eyes, and very trim but manly figure. She was smitten, and no amount of persuading could change her mind. They were married when she was nineteen—on a cold, wintry day in February. They lived with my other grandparents for a few months and then found the home that I lived in until I was nine years old. Then, we moved to another house, which was a single house, and we had a much larger yard. My mom would plant flowers outside in a circular flower garden: sweet peas, gladioli, and petunias, among others.

I loved looking at the beautiful flowers, and despite what she had to do each day, she always found time to give us beauty through our surroundings.

We had a little broom closet on the back porch, which I made into a playhouse with a little table, chairs, my dolls, and a wonderful tea set. We would play "tea party" often, and I loved being in the playhouse and acted as if it were a house of my own.

We played many games in the yard—including hide-and-go-seek, kick-the-can, red rover, and other games—with my cousins and friends.

It was a wonderful time. It was full of fun in the summer, and in the winter, we sledded down the side yard, built snowmen, and had snowball fights. We had a nice group of cousins and friends, and I will never forget those days.

Fear crippled me sometimes, and that is why it was so important for me to gain relief through the childhood fun of playing.

My father raised us up with many fears, like "Don't go swimming—you'll drown" and "Don't ride far in a car—you'll have an accident," and he told us of children dying at an early age.

All of these things made us all fearful of life. Coupled with some teachings I had heard about committing "mortal sins," I was fearful about committing sins to the point that I became scrupulous.

I would go to confession once a month, and I would be so fearful in the church before I even went into the confessional that my body would be soaked with sweat. I was afraid I *had* committed a mortal sin or more, and I went over and over things in my mind to see if I *had* committed them. I would tell the priest that I was confessing these things just in case I had committed them.

I would go so far as to walk down the street and shake my head back and forth so that I wouldn't have any bad thoughts in my mind. I wish I had talked this over with someone, especially my mother, but I was too ashamed, and I kept everything buried within me, and the fear never really left. It was just masked by other things I had been doing, like coloring in my coloring books, playing with my paper dolls, and playing board games with my sister and brother.

I was always dreading going to confession, and that dread stayed in my heart. That is why I liked the diversion of not thinking about it all for a time.

I would go to Holy Communion while always doubting if I were "in the state of grace," as they called it, and free from sins.

Sometimes I would just sit on the pew and not go—even when I was in church with my classmates—as I wasn't sure if I *was* "in the state of grace." I am sure my classmates wondered what terrible things I had done if I thought I should not receive Holy Communion.

This went on for many years, and I was always wondering about sin and fearing it. In my own mind, God the Father was not portrayed as a loving, kind father. He was more like a judge of all our thoughts, words, and actions. I prayed, but I didn't have the real knowledge of how wonderful God really is. I learned this at a later time in my life.

Our second house was a two-story brown-shingled house with a big front porch and a back porch with a broom closet. We would sit on the front porch in the summer and play board games: checkers, Parcheesi, and Monopoly, among others. We had a little brown-and-white male dog that we named Rags.

Rags would sit on the front porch with us—usually sitting by my brother, sister, and me—and we would play the games.

I was about ten years old at the time, and as we were playing, Rags ran after a car that was passing by on the road adjacent to our sidewalk. The car couldn't stop in time and hit Rags, and he whimpered and then passed away. I was hysterical and ran into the house while crying loudly. My dad had been upstairs and sleeping at the time, and he came running down the stairs to see what had happened. He went out and removed Rags from the road. The driver of the car had gotten out of his car and told us how sorry he was. He offered to get us another dog, but my mother told him that he didn't have to do that.

My brother, Jimmy, and Barbara were upset too, of course, and we just cried and cried.

Later, we got two beagle dogs, Mojo and Bozo, and we had fun playing with them, and they followed us around in the yard.

Our house didn't have hot water, so my mother had to heat up the water on the coal stove for doing the dishes and our baths, which were taken in a metal tub in the kitchen as our home didn't have a bathroom. When I was thirteen years old, we had to move to a steelmaking city in West Virginia as my dad developed silicosis (black lung) from the coal mines and couldn't work in them anymore. It was a change from our hometown, but we adjusted, and one of the things that we *did* have was a bathroom. I kept cleaning the bathroom as I was so excited to have one.

I had always prayed to find a good husband someday, and as it turned out, my husband-to-be lived on the next street over, and we were married when we were twenty-two years old. He is a very good and kind man.

We have three grown children, four grandchildren, and two great-grandchildren, who are all kind, loving, caring, and compassionate, and we are so proud of them all and have been blessed so greatly by God.

It took a while for me to really *trust* in *God the Father and Jesus, his Son.* It took a while for me to get over the distortions of the scrupulosity. Finally, I "saw" *God in all his magnificence, splendor, kindness, love, caring, and mercy for us all.* I understood a *new God, a faithful God, and a loving, caring God. I understood Jesus, his Son, and the awesome gift of the Holy Spirit.*

It is said that when a man asked Jesus to heal his son who was at home, Jesus said to the man, "Go thy way, your son is healed."

The Bible states, "And he started for home."

He *"started for home" while trusting in Jesus's words and in God, his Father, who sent Jesus to earth.*

As I trust him and love him with all my heart and know how good he is,

I too, after praying and asking God for all our needs, am "starting for home."

As it turned out, my grandmother was right to be cautious about my father as he ended up having a drinking problem and had outbursts of temper that would be upsetting to our whole family. He was sometimes rough with my mother and used angry, abusive language with us also. He was a man with two sides to him. He would make our childhood swings and make cowboy chaps with deer hide. He loved wearing cowboy hats and western belt buckles and watched Randolph Scott western movies. He also loved to sing songs in the evenings with us. He would start singing, and we would all join in. He loved the songs, "Oh, My Darling Clementine," "You Are My Sunshine," and "Red River Valley." The other side of him was a very angry man. We learned that in his childhood, he was treated differently than his siblings and was made to go to work in the coal mines at the age of ten. His parents told him that he would have to quit school, after only going to the fourth grade, and go to work with his father on his father's shifts to help out with the family income. None of the other brothers had to do the same, and he even had an older brother who continued with his education. My dad also told us things like when he was little, he wasn't given money to ride the carousel at the carnival when it came to town, and his other siblings were, so he would run alongside of it, around and around, and pretend that he was riding one of the horses. Another thing was that he gave his whole paycheck from the mines to his mother, and she would give him a quarter back, and that was all. My dad told us that his food and water bucket was so heavy for him to carry that he would drag it along the ground and then go into the mines with his father; he was only ten. I had resentment for my father for many years, especially for his treatment of my mother. She was a saint; she tried to keep our home with normalcy, always trying to have big dinners for holidays and cooking and baking and serving delicious meals for all of us. You would not know from looking at her that she had this problem with him, and she remained cheerful with us and even gave me a beautiful ninth birthday party, which had a Valentine's Day theme as my birthday is in February. We invited all my classmates, and she even thought of having a Valentine King and Queen crowned at the party.

My mother was known for her wonderful pastries and her Jell-O cake, which my cousins still talk about because she served them with one whenever they visited on Sunday afternoons. One of my cousins wrote to me that she will never forget my mother making her a beautiful blue dress for her graduation. She always treated everyone who came to our home so kindly and was loved by them all.

As I grew up and got married and had my own children, my resentment started to fade, and I thought of my dad enduring what he did as a child, and I thought that it did have an effect on him; he was not even able to have any say about the things that were done to him. I did forgive him in his later years; he must have not really known how he could cope and sort out the bad things that were done to him, and these were just kept inside his heart for many years.

My dad, at the age of eighty-six, developed cancer and had a stroke, and he couldn't speak. He passed away on a Saint Patrick's Day while lying in a hospital bed with his family all around him. I was sitting at his bedside and holding his hand, and I leaned over to speak closer to his ear and told him, "Go to Jesus," and he did.

OH, MY DARLING CLEMENTINE

"In a cavern, in a canyon,

Excavating for a mine,

Dwelt a miner, forty-niner,

And his daughter, Clementine."

PART 4

"THE LORD IS MY SHEPHERD, I SHALL NOT WANT. HE LEADS ME BESIDE THE STILL WATERS."

GOOD TIDINGS

"Behold, I bring you good tidings of great joy, which shall be to all people."

"Good tidings," the angel said to shepherds down below. Angels in the sky brought news of *great joy* to *all people*!

There have never been such tidings, for *a savior was born*—for the *world*—a *savior* to *take away sins*—*a savior* to *redeem* the *world*!

God announced the message through his angels in the sky. What were the angels thinking, and how were they rejoicing and giving their love to all?

What a day for the angels!

What a day for us!

JOY TO THE WORLD

Joy to the *world*!

The Lord is *come*!

Let earth *receive* her *king*!

We do!

I AM THE GOOD SHEPHERD

"I am the Good Shepherd. A shepherd lays down His
life for the sheep" (John 10:11, NIV).

Jesus gave his life for all of us. We are his sheep, and he is *our shepherd*.
He laid down his life so that we might have eternal life. We come into
his fold by accepting what he has done for us.

"We accept, sweet Jesus, all that you have done for us. We want to
be *yours forever*! *Amen*!"

LAZARUS AND THE RICH MAN

Jesus, the rich man who had died wanted *Lazarus* to come back from the dead and warn his brothers. He was told, "If they won't pay attention to Moses and the prophets, they won't listen even if someone comes back from the dead" (Luke 16:31, CEV).

Jesus, we are sorry for being like the rich man when we are indifferent to the suffering around us.

Open our eyes to see,

To feel, and

To do

Whatever you would have us do.

Amen.

THE TEN LEPERS

Jesus, the lepers went away, didn't they, after you had healed them? They ran to tell the priest that they were healed. Only one came back, a Samaritan, to thank you and praise you for all (Luke 17:16).

Jesus, help us be like the Samaritan; help us thank you and praise you for all.

Jesus, thank you. We thank you with all our hearts for all that you have done for us. We thank you with all our hearts for *you*! Amen.

Luke 5:29–32

JESUS IN THE HOME OF LEVI

Jesus, when you were in the home of Levi, everyone was reclining around the table. You looked around. There were tax collectors, teachers of the law, sinners, the shoddy, the unkempt, and the rich, who were clothed in fine garments.

Your disciples were there also, and they were asked by the scribes and the Pharisees, "Why do you eat and drink with tax collectors and sinners?"

Your answer to them was "Healthy people do not need a doctor, but sick people do. I did not come to invite the righteous, but sinners to repentance."

Jesus, you looked around. They are your little sheep. They are all yours. You love them. You clean them up in your mind. You see them as they *will* be, not as they are now. You know the good deep within. You know the possibility. You know what it will take.

Jesus, look at us. Are *we* possibilities? You look beyond our sins, as you did to them, and see us as we will be. Cleanse us of our sins—now and forever. Amen.

THE WIDOW'S SON

Jesus, the widow of Nain was crying. Her son had died; he was her only child. Tears glistened in her eyes and rolled down her cheeks. She was bent and stooped but turned to look up at you—a world of sorrow in her eyes. Her sobs could be heard audibly, and you turned and looked deep into her eyes. You were sorry that she had such grief. You wanted to take her grief away. You said to her,

"Do not weep" (Luke 7:13–14).

Then you touched the stretcher and said, "Young man, I say to you, arise."

The man sat up and began to speak, and you presented him to his mother.

Jesus, will you say to *us*, "*Arise*—arise from fear, from brokenness, from despair, from self-pity, from depression, and from grief and *trust and obey* and go on your way, *rejoicing* in *truth*. Children, my children, I say to *you, arise!*"

THE DENIAL OF PETER

Jesus, Peter denied *you* three times. You said, "Peter, before the rooster crows, you will deny three times that you know me" (Matt. 26:34).

Jesus, you turned and looked at Peter. It was a look of compassion, tenderness, and love—a look of forgiveness.

Jesus, help us. We too have denied you through our doubts, fears, worries, and anxieties. We have denied you through our indifference to you, through our lassitude, and through our not trusting in your love, mercy, and forgiveness.

Jesus, help us. We are sorry. Help us proclaim you, acknowledge you, and trust in you. Help us bring you honor through the lives that we lead. We believe in you. We believe in your love. We accept you as *our* savior. Amen.

A MEDITATION: SIMON OF CYRENE HELPS JESUS TO CARRY HIS CROSS

Jesus, they enlisted Simon of Cyrene to help you carry the cross. We then notice him, a man of your stature, standing there with a younger boy.

They said "You, come and help!" and gave him no choice. He was afraid to refuse. It was all so intense—the crowd pressing to see, changing their positions as the *man* moved along the road. The crowd was looking at *you*, dear Jesus. They saw your brown hair—shoulder-length and matted with blood. They saw your robe, more red than white, soaked in the blood of the wounds on your body. They looked at your eyes—so deep and so penetrating—and wondered,

"Who is this man?"

The soldiers had their whips, ready to find something to do with them. Simon approached the cross. It was dirty work, but he had to do it. He did not want to antagonize the soldiers who commanded him. *He* looked at you.

What have you done? he thought to himself. *You must have done something terribly wrong.*

Simon took the cross with the help of the soldiers. Two of them straightened it up on his back.

How odd this is—to carry the cross for someone that I don't even know, he thought.

Jesus, help *me* carry *my* cross each day, and when I can't carry it anymore, send me *my* Simon of Cyrene until I can go on again.

The soldiers roughly pushed you, Jesus, thinking that you should be able to move faster without the weight of the cross.

You looked behind. You looked at Simon.

Down through the ages, you thought, *Simon will be remembered. They will tell of this man who walked behind me and carried my load. They will tell of a man named Simon of Cyrene, who helped me carry my cross* (Matt. 27:32).

The man's eyes looked at you. You said to him in your heart, "Oh, Simon, I love you too.

I am doing this for you too, Simon.

You are gaining something by carrying *my* cross.

The cross will be used to give *you* paradise, Simon of Cyrene. You only have to say *yes!*"

JESUS IS NAILED TO THE CROSS

Jesus, the soldiers roughly pulled your garments from *you*. They were rough because they were in a hurry. They wanted to finish the task at hand. You were just another body to them—another crucifixion. They were used to the nails, the cross, and the spear. They did not *see*, did they, Jesus? They did not know that what they were doing at that hour would be told in history.

You are history, Jesus. What you do will live on forever. People will be talking, thinking, and writing about you and these soldiers for thousands of years. They were making their *own place in history*.

"The soldiers nailed Jesus to a cross and gambled to see who would get His clothes" (Matt. 27:35).

They did not know you, Jesus, but we know.

We *know* who you are, and we call you *King, Lord*, and *Savior*. We call you the *Savior of the World—the Holy One of God*.

Your clothes were on the ground, dear Jesus, and you lay there upon the cross—nailed to it for the sins of all humanity.

Take us, dear Jesus, and strip away any attachment to sin in our lives.

Clothe us in righteousness and holiness with *your* righteousness and holiness.

Cover us with your grace and truth forever. Amen.

CHRIST LOVED US AND GAVE HIMSELF UP FOR US

"CHRIST LOVED US AND GAVE HIMSELF
UP FOR US" (Eph. 5:2, NIV).

Christ loved *us*! Imagine that—the Creator's Son, full of power and love, came and *gave himself* willingly for us!

Did he *have* to do this? *No*, but he loved *us* so much; he loved people who weren't even in existence yet.

What love! He gave himself up for us! We love you, dear Jesus! Amen!

FOR GOD SO LOVED THE WORLD

"For God so loved the world that he GAVE His only begotten SON, that whosoever would believe on Him, He would have ETERNAL life" (John 3:16).

I believe!

"In THIS is love, not that We loved GOD, but that HE LOVED US, and sent HIS SON to be the ATONING SACRIFICE for OUR SINS" (1 John 4:10, NET).

Jesus atoned for all our sins. I can be free of my sins by accepting what *Jesus* did for *me*!

I accept!

THE LOVE OF JESUS

Father, we offer you the precious blood of Jesus, which was shed in his sufferings for all humanity to save the world.

Do this now, kind Father. Look not on our sins but *look* at *Jesus* and *his love*.

This will keep us *safe* in the *name* of *Jesus*. Amen.

A MEDITATION: JESUS IS PLACED IN THE TOMB

Joseph of Arimathea and Nicodemus carried you into the tomb, dear Jesus (John 19:38). Your robe was white—a burial cloth—and you were wrapped together with the spices. Women were weeping, and your mother looked into the tomb. It would be your resting place only for a short time. She knew it would end. You promised.

The soldiers were watching to make sure nothing went awry. You were carefully laid down on the stone burial place. There were tears in the eyes of your mother and the other women. They were still weeping. Joseph of Arimathea and his helper smoothed out the burial cloth.

There was no sound but a sob and then some rustling, and then you were laid to rest.

Joseph gave you a glance—a glance of disbelief and the pain of a broken heart. Your mother's sobs were quiet and hushed as she tenderly told you goodbye for a short time.

She kissed your face and then straightened the cloth on your shoulders and left the tomb.

But, Jesus, you were soon resurrected. Your eyes were closed, but your eyes saw heaven.

Help *us* see heaven with our eyes.

Help us see beyond the pain and death of earth—

a new resurrection—

A resurrection for us all.

Help us see *you* clothed in heaven's garments—

Alive, beautiful, and well.

Take us there someday, Jesus.

We want to be with you forever. Amen.

The tomb lay in darkness.

The stone had been rolled to cover the entrance of the tomb.

There was only darkness, but there would be *light*.

The *light* is coming forever! Amen!

THE ASCENSION

Jesus, you said, "All authority has been given to Me in heaven and on earth. Go therefore and make disciples of all the nations, baptizing them in the Name of the Father, and of the Son, and of the Holy Spirit, teaching them to observe all that I have commanded you, and lo, I am with you, always, EVEN to the end of the age" (Matt. 28:18–20, NKJV).

"He lifted up His hands and blessed them and was parted from them and carried up into heaven" (Luke 24:50–51, NKJV).

Jesus, lift *us* up to you. Lift us up away from any harm. We are in danger if we allow fear, depression, self-pity, and despair to beat down our souls and spirits and keep us chained to these thoughts.

Jesus, help us rise above our pain and anguish and see you! We have been hurt, dearest Jesus. Heal the broken places, heal the wounds in our hearts, and make us whole with your truth and love.

We are sorry for hurting you with our sins. You are our God and King. You are our Ruler. *Be* a ruler now, dear Lord, and take us safely under your wings forever.

PENTECOST

Jesus, tongues of fire appeared above the twelve apostles and your mother (Acts 2:1–3). The room was quiet, and then the wind rushed in and the tongues appeared over everyone gathered there.

The Holy Spirit had been given.

Oh, bathe *us* in your Holy Spirit.

Set a tongue of fire above each of our heads and over all the earth.

Come, Holy Spirit. Envelop, renew, strengthen, and confirm all the world in your grace. Amen.

THE MERCY OF GOD

The mercy of God covers the earth with the redeeming blood of Jesus. Jesus paid the price so that we could all have eternal life and that our sins would be washed away. There is no one who is beyond the mercy of God when they repent and come back to him.

God's mercy fills the earth as soothing rain and as the peaceful waters washing away the sins of the world. The mercy comes from the cross as an ever-flowing stream and envelops the entire world.

We can all stand beneath the cross today and receive this mercy. It is for everyone! All that we have to do is *ask*!

Father, we ask for your mercy over all the earth. Amen.

PART 5

"LET THE LITTLE CHILDREN COME TO ME, FOR OF SUCH IS THE KINGDOM OF HEAVEN."

WE ARE HARD-PRESSED

"We are hard-pressed on every side, but not crushed. We are perplexed, but not in despair, persecuted, but not forsaken, struck down, but not destroyed, always carrying about in the body the dying of our Lord Jesus Christ, that the life of Jesus also may be manifested in us" (2 Cor. 4:8–10, NKJV).

We *are* hard-pressed on every side, dear Lord, but we are not crushed! Thank you and praise you forever! Amen.

OUR HEARTS REJOICE

"In Him our hearts rejoice, for we trust in His Holy Name" (Ps.33:21, NIV).

Our hearts *do* rejoice, for we trust in his holy name. The name of God is so powerful, trusting, wonderful, and almighty. We have a God who *can do all things*!

There is nothing he cannot do!

And so, our hearts *can* rejoice. God *can* save, help, cure, and enter our lives through a beautiful way! We have God forever!

ALL THINGS

"I can do ALL things in HIM who strengthens me." We *can* do *all things in God.*

There is *nothing* on earth that we *can't* do because *Jesus* is with us and gives us *his* strength.

Jesus is my strength!

JESUS'S LOVE AND GRACE

Jesus, I give you my heart and my soul. I ask to always be in your grace and in your love. I receive you as my Lord and Savior. You are my Savior forever. Thank you, Jesus. Amen.

I WILL BLESS YOU

"I WILL BLESS YOU ... AND YOU WILL BE A BLESSING" (Gen. 12:2, NIV).

"I will bless you." God *will* bless and promises a blessing. We are blessed when we believe, when we trust, and when we love.

Then we *are* a blessing to ourselves and to others and to God!

THE GOD OF HOPE

"May the God of hope, fill you with all joy and peace in believing."

God *is* a God of hope. There is *always* hope in God. He fills us with all *joy* and *peace*. *He* gives us the way to *trust* Him, to *rely* on him, and to choose to give *all* our problems to him. Then, joy and peace can come!

We know we have *hope* in God.

Take *everything*, dear Lord. Take all my concerns, worries, needs—everything!

Then, I shall be filled with your *peace* and *joy*! *Amen.*

GIVE THANKS

"I give thanks to my God at every remembrance of you" (Phil 1:3, NABRE).

I give thanks to my God for every remembrance of my husband, my children, my grandchildren and great-grandchildren, my mother, my father, my sisters and brother, and all my friends, loved ones, and the people in my life.

I thank God for *all* of them.

So many blessings, so many gifts, and so much enjoyment and happiness for us all!

Thank you, God, for all!

Amen.

RESPECT

Father, teach us to respect all your children. *We* are yours—all of us. We live, breathe, work, and play in your heart. Never let us let you down by any disrespect of others. When we look at anyone in any other way, it is sin. Oh, Father, make us not sin. Make us respect others by instilling in us your respect. You love us as we are. You look beyond our faults and weaknesses and see the good underneath. Help us lift people up and not tear them down.

Give us your arms! Amen.

A PRAYER

Holy Spirit, we surrender all our thoughts, our words, our actions, our feelings, and our situations to you. Heal us from our many wounds. Help us remain steadfast in your Word. Heal us of any wrongful thinking. Give each of us a new mind and a new heart. We ask for your gift of fortitude to strengthen us. In Jesus's name, we pray. Amen.

PETITION

Dear Father, *my* needs are many.

I present this one especially to your care.

I place this in your heart.

Hear my petition, kind Father,

And grant my request in Jesus's name. Amen.

PURITY

Father, we need to be pure. Help us be pure in our hearts, our minds, our souls, and our spirits. Touch us with your purity. Enflame our souls with the touch of your heart. Your heart is total purity.

Make us pure by the light of your love. Burn in us the emblem of your love so that all love would be of you and that all that we will think, feel, or act upon will measure up to the love in your heart.

We ask this in Jesus's name. Amen.

PRAYING

Father, teach me to pray. Prayer is your voice speaking to us and our voices speaking to you. Let me use my voice for prayer often. Help me call upon you during the moment I need help. Help me recognize your voice. Help me use prayer as a two-way communication with you. Let me listen, speak, and wait. May I use prayer for adoration, thanksgiving, petition, and loving you for all your majesty, power, and help. May I always wait until I do know your will for my life, and then let me do your will always. Amen.

CALLED BY NAME

"I have called you by name. You are mine."

God calls us by our names. He says that we are *his*! The Creator *knows our names* and wants us to be *his—in love, service, and truth*. We *are* yours, *Holy God*! *Amen*!

GOD'S GIFT

"Thank God for this gift, HIS gift. No language can praise it enough" (2 Cor. 9:15).

We thank you, God, for this gift—the gift of your Son coming down from heaven for us—to save our souls. No language *can* praise it enough. The *gift* is *ours*. We only have to say yes to *accept* this gift into our hearts, and then, *we can praise in whatever language we speak.*

We praise you, Father, for your gift!

Amen.

THIS IS THE DAY THE LORD HAS MADE

"This is the day the Lord has made—

Let us rejoice and be glad" (Ps. 118:24, ESV). Let us rejoice for God *is* in *control*—

Of *all*!

Thank you, Father. Amen.

TRUST IN THE LORD AND DO GOOD

"TRUST IN THE LORD AND DO GOOD" (Ps. 37:3, NIV).

Dear Father, help me trust in you and do good. Give my heart trust in all that you do and give it to me for my whole life.

I trust you, Father. Help me do good always and forever. Amen!

MY CUP

"My cup runs over" (Ps. 23:5, NKJV).

My cup runs over with blessings. God has richly blessed me and all my family.

Your cup runs over with *all the blessings of God!* He is *good.* He *never forsakes,* and he only *loves.*

Thank you, Father God,

For all our blessings.

Thank you for my cup running over—

For every blessing of my life. Amen!

YOU ARE MY GOD

"You are my God! My future is in Your hands" (Ps. 31:14).

You are my God! My future *is* in *your hands*! I give you all my life. I give you my love. *Everything* I have, all that I do, and all that is mine are *yours*!

All my days lie in your hands. Do *all* in *me—forever*! Amen!

FOR HE COMMANDS HIS ANGELS

"For He commands His angels with regard to you, to guard you WHEREVER you go" (Ps. 91:11, NABRE).

He *commands* his angels for all of us; he commands them to *guard* us wherever *we go*! Angels are all around us. Angels are behind us. Angels keep us safe. If we *could see them*, we would *never be afraid*. They *are* at *our side*. Thank you, angels everywhere. Keep us all safe!

A life lived with angels— Guarding, loving, protecting Me and you!

A WOMAN WHO HONORS THE LORD

"A woman who honors the Lord deserves to be praised" (Prov. 31:30, CEV).

A woman who honors God *is* worthy of being praised. She gives God worship, respect, glory, honor, praise, and all her love. She lives every day of her life in rejoicing in the magnificence and awesomeness of God and in humility of heart, knowing that he loves us for no reason of ours *but to love, for he is love for all—forever!*

GOD ARMS HIM WITH STRENGTH

"God arms me with strength and keeps my way secure"
(Ps. 18:32, NIV).

He does make our way *secure*. That is so true! Thank you, dear God, for making and keeping my way secure.

I love you, God—forever and ever!

BELOVED, I PRAY THAT ALL MAY GO WELL WITH YOU

"Beloved, I pray that all may go well with you and that you may be in good health as it goes well with your soul" (3 John 1:2, ESV).

What a beautiful prayer! To pray that all may go well—that we may be in good health and well. Having these things makes our lives happy and whole. Thank you, Father, for all!

CLOUDS

When I was a little girl, I would look up at the clouds and wonder, hope, and dream. I would see shapes of many things: boats, animals, hearts, and angels looking down.

The white puffy clouds showed me that there is more to life than our hectic pace. Clouds give us a sense of purpose, and with their ethereal beauty, they show us that there *is* more to life than making money or having power or achieving our own ambitions.

Clouds bring us to our knees so that we know that *God lives, God cares, and God gives beauty and majesty over all the earth.*

"The works of God are manifold," and when we look up at the clouds, we see a part of God's heart—a part that is displayed for us all!

FATHER'S LOVE AND HOPE

Father, when I think of you, I think of love and hope. You are always there to help, to heal, and to care. I give you my love, my heart, and my pain. I give you the answer to my problems. You know what to do. Help me know what to do also. I give you all my love and all my truth. I need you to help me do the right thing and think the right thoughts and stay always in your will. Your will is my safety. Help me be safe. Amen.

THE LORD IS GOOD

"For the Lord is good, His unfailing love continues forever, and His faithfulness continues to each generation."

The Lord's *unfailing* love continues forever to all generations!

The Lord's love is *faithful* to *all* of us. It continues forever! What a gift from the eternal God! His love never comes to an end!

His faithfulness comes down to *each* generation. The Lord is good!

A God of love forever to each generation!

Praise to you, Almighty God, who continues in unfailing love for me and for all!

THE TRUST OF GOD

]If we trust someone, we know that they care and that they will always do what is *best* for us. *God* is worthy of trust. He fills the earth with his gifts. He gives us his love, grace, and mercy. He gives us all that we would ever need.

The trust of God is an awakening in our souls that makes us give ourselves totally and completely to *his* care. We can *accept* his will for us with a grateful heart, knowing that *his will* for us is the *best*. We can safely put our hands in his and say,

"Father, we trust you. We give you our hearts, lives, and concerns.

Do what is *best* for us. Amen."

BE STILL

"Be still and know that I am God."

Be still and *know* that he is God!

We are to *trust* him, not try to force things or make *our* will be done.

To be *still* is to be silent in love, trust, hope, and security. *He is God!*

That is all we need to believe and know!

God can do all things!

Thank you, Father, for all!

THE LORD IS ONE

Oh, Lord, you are one with all of us.

Your heart beats with ours and becomes one giant heart of love over all the earth.

You have made us one with all our brothers and sisters. We are joined in our sorrows and joys and in all our needs. We are one with the continuity of the universe.

All things, all creatures—everything that has been created speaks the glory of the Creator, and that is you.

COURAGE

Father, I need courage. Give me yours. You do not fear. You know—truly know—the way. Give me the way, Father. Give me your help. Amen.

LOVE

Father, your way is love—only love. Teach us this love. To love is to bring you honor. Oh, make us honor you with our love. Make love our aim—to love and love and love. Show us this way to love in Jesus's name. Amen.

LIFE

Father, you are life. Teach us this life. Give us your life. Give us a part of you. Then we shall be safe. Satan wants to destroy our lives through self-pity, depression, and hate. Oh, make us calm in you. Give our lives meaning, direction, and purpose. Give our lives you! You are the butterflies and the wind in the trees. You are the flowers, the birds, and the hills.

You are the direction for everyone's life if only we allow it. We need you, Father. We accept life from your hands. We accept the praise for everything that occurs in our lives. We accept you! Amen.

SUFFERING

Father, why do we suffer? I think I know. Suffering is a part of life—
but only a part. Joy will come in the end. Joy is a part of life too. I pray
for the strength, the courage, and the perseverance to wait for the joy.
I pray for joy. Amen.

SACRAMENT

Jesus, you are a sacrament to me—one that covers the earth. You give us your body to eat and your blood to drink. You are the Eucharist in my heart. You are the life-giving bread and the cup of salvation.

I hold you in my heart. Reign there with total blessing. You are Lord forever in me. Amen.

JOY

Father, teach us your joy. Make joy the reason for our lives; make us give joy to others. Make us apostles of joy. Make joy our gift to those around us. Joy is the bearer of your grace.

Grant that we may bring this gift of joy and grace to every soul that we encounter. Let them feel the joy we feel in our hearts. Let them accept this joy and live with this joy forever! Amen.

DEAR FATHER

Dear Father,

I thank you for being *who* you are—kind and loving.

You look at me and love me.

You never *stop* loving me.

Help me truly love *you* in return.

Help me *never* stop looking at *you*!

I love *you*, Father. Amen.

CHANT OF LOVE

My heart sings of your beauty, oh Lord.

The birds chant their praises to you.

The flowers bow their heads in deepest adoration.

The sea calls to *you* in the thunderous roaring of the waves.

The rainbow proclaims your faithfulness,

And I—I can only look with awe and wonder at what you have made

And see all of this—

See *you*—and feel your love.

MAJESTY

Oh, Lord, *you* are majestic in all your ways,

From mountains high

To lowly glens,

To rushing streams,

To quiet pools,

To star-filled nights,

And snowy skies,

To reddened sunsets

With fiery glow

To light of morning

And evening shade—

It is all

That God has made!

FOR ME

The horrendous death—
Spikes pounded into your hands and feet—
A crown of thorns
And lashes wet all over your body.

What creature would wish to endure this?
And yet you stayed,
Still and motionless,
While it was done.

Your heart looked away
From all—deleting
Anything that needed to be done—
And you stayed and suffered

For *me*!
Thank you,
Jesus, from *me*!
I love you, Jesus.

WHAT I COULD HAVE DONE

I could have done, I would have done, I should have done—

But did I?

I could have stayed, I would have stayed, I should have stayed—

But did I?

I could have cared, I would have cared, I should have cared—

But did I?

I could have gone, I would have gone, I should have gone—

But did I?

I could have given, I should have given, I would have given—

But did I?

I could have loved, I should have loved, I would have loved—

But did I?

I could have prayed, I would have prayed, I should have prayed—

But did I?

Was I too busy, too uncaring, too soft To stake my claim—

To do all things in God's sweet name?

Did I wait too long? Did I heed the throng To go along

With the times of the day? That there would still *be* time,

And I would not miss my chance sublime? But was there?

Did I think that there Would be time to care? But was there?

A CHILD OF GOD

A child of God. "How great is the love that the Father has lavished on us, that we should be called children of God."

God's love! On us!

To make us *his children*!

A child of the Almighty Father!

We are! We are his!

MAY THE GOD OF HOPE FILL YOU

"May the God of hope fill you with all joy and peace as
you trust in Him, so that you may overflow with hope
by the power of the Holy Spirit" (Rom. 15:13, NIV).

Joy and peace come as we *trust* in God, and then we overflow with *hope*
by the Holy Spirit, according to St. Paul. We need to pray for *trust* in
all things so that we may *have joy* and *peace*. Trusting God takes love,
obedience, and respect, knowing that he is *good and will do all things
for our good*. Trusting God is knowing that he is God and loves us and
wants the best for us.

*We pray to trust you, Heavenly Father, in all things in our lives. We
give you our lives and ask that you take care of all for us, for we do trust in
your love, your care, and your providence in our lives. Thank you, Father,
for giving us your joy and peace. Amen!*

HONOR

Father, you are honorable. Help us be honorable in our dealings with others. Help us be honest, kind, caring, and respectful. Never let us deceive or manipulate. Show us your honor, Father.

You speak truth always. Tell us truth, Father. Say to us, "It is only in truth, in peace, and in justice that we can find honor."

Give us this in Jesus's name. Amen.

CARING

Father, I don't care enough. I don't love enough. Give me your caring, Father. Somehow I got lost, lost amid my own cares, and lost the real caring. I care for others, Father, to live the life you want me to live and the life I want to live. Caring for others will make me whole. Oh, make me whole. Amen.

THE LORD IS KING

A king you are—rich in glory, rich in love.

I kneel before your throne in deepest love and adoration.

I whisper my petitions, knowing that even a king as great as you hears the heartbeat of a child

And that you will hear me, and what is more soothing to my ears will answer with love.

I have no fear that what I ask will be laid aside and forgotten,

For you have promised, "Ask and you shall receive," and while asking, I believe.

LIGHT

Father, give me the light. I need the light. Help me see that the road is leading somewhere. Help me see you at the end of the road. Then, I will be calm and at peace. Amen.

PEACE

Father, we need peace. Our souls yearn for peace. Show us the way to peace. Give us your blessing so that even amid the storm, peace will prevail. Let us rest on your heart. Let us calm the storm by having total trust in your goodness, mercy, and help. Father, make our hearts rest in your peace. Amen.

PERSEVERANCE

Father, give us the perseverance we need to wait for the right. Help us see that you have everything in your hands. You need our prayers to pray for the right. We pray, Father. Amen.

ABANDONMENT

Father, I release all into your hands. I accept all—all that you would choose to give. I accept all the workings of your will. You are the light; give me the light. Take me out of the darkness. Take me and make me whole in Jesus's name. Amen.

QUIET

Father, I need to be quiet. I need to be still. Make me still, Father. Breathe upon me your stillness. Allow me to wait—to wait for the dawn. The dawn will come if I wait. Amen.

COURTESIES

Father, teach us the little courtesies of the day. Let us fill one another's lives with small pleasantries. Let us be kind and courteous and treat one another with love.

Love is beautiful, Father. Help us love. Let no one leave our home with a feeling of not being shown love. Let us extend the simple kindnesses of courtesy to all we meet. Amen.

SICKNESS

Father, I am sick. Heal me. Take the pain and use it for another. I offer this pain for them to be made whole. Help me learn and grow through this time of pain. Help me use it for your glory. Amen.

CLIMBING MOUNTAINS

Father, the hills are steep, the way is bleak, and the light is dim. I am weary, hurting, and sick.

Heal the sickness—the sickness within. Help me climb the mountains with you.

You are the sun; give *me* the sun, Father. Shed light upon my heart. I love you, Father. You are my God.

Be God now, Father, and make me climb with you. Make me reach the top and give rest to my soul. Amen.

HOLINESS

Oh, God, make me holy. Breathe upon me the gifts of your Spirit. Give me all the graces—the gifts that will make me holy. I need holiness from you, Father.

Send your Holy Spirit to free me from all my sins. It is by the blood of Jesus on the cross that we are set free. Make me free. Amen.

ADORATION

Father, I pray for you to be loved as you deserve to be loved, praised as you deserve to be praised, and honored as you deserve to be honored and adored throughout all the ages. Amen!

PRAYERS

Father, you have always been there for us. Thank you, Father, for your love.

Father, I place this intention in your heart. I ask for it to be blessed. Amen.

Father, bless me; my family; all our friends, acquaintances, and work associates; our country; and the world. Amen.

Jesus, I need your help to do your will in my life. Amen.

Jesus, the children and young people need your help. Help them to be good, to do good, and to serve you as their Lord and Savior. Amen.

Father, whenever I prayed, you always gave me help. Thank you, Father. Amen.

Jesus, I love you.

Jesus, I pray that all the sick will be helped. Heal them, bless them, and give them comfort, peace, and joy. Help them feel your nearness, blessing, and love. Amen.

Jesus, I am sorry for all my sins. I repent of them, and I ask for help not to sin again. I love you, Jesus. Amen.

Jesus, help all of us who need your help. I pray for all of us to receive your grace and help in all our difficulties. Amen.

Father, bless all of us in our family to receive salvation, our loved ones, and all the world. Amen.

JESUS

Jesus, give us strength to do all, to bear all, to trust all, and to allow all in your will. Jesus, we need your help. Amen.

Father, I offer my pain to you. Bring me your healing. Amen. Father, the world is in chaos. Free it from all evil. Amen.

Father, we need the light. *Send* the light. Amen.

Father, I place all my cares on your lap. Hold them, Father. Bless each one and give me help, love, and peace. I love you, Father. Amen.

Father, I love you. You have always taken care of me. You gave me life, love, and happiness. You give us everything on earth. Thank you, Father, for *you*! Amen.

PRAYERS

Dear Father, I pray to trust you with all my life. *All* my life is yours forever! Amen.

Jesus, I place this intention in your heart.
Answer it in love. Amen.

Jesus, we love you—always love you. Amen.

Jesus, I pray for the soul who will not be saved. I pray for that soul *to* be saved. Amen.

Jesus, I love you. Take care of me. Amen.

Dear Jesus, help me learn all that I must learn in your will. Amen.

Dear Father, I pray to pray more with trust, peace, and love. Help me, Father. Amen.

Father, I love you always and forever. Amen.

Jesus, say the Word. The Word is *truth*. Bring *truth*. Amen.

PRAYERS

When I was a little girl, I prayed,
"Father, keep us safe—all my family and the world.
Father, I pray this now.
Keep us safe. Amen.

"Jesus, vanquish the evil by the Word.
Jesus, say the Word. Amen.

"Father, I belong to you—now and forever. Amen.

"Father, I need help in this situation.
Help me, Father. Amen.

"Jesus, there is so much that is *not* love.
Make it into love. Amen."

Dear Father,

The world is in chaos. The world needs you! Father, come!

Father, my heart is heavy. I need you. I need your grace and your blessing. I need to feel your presence, which brings peace and joy.

Thank you, Father. Amen.

The world needs the touch of your hand, Father. Give us your touch. Amen.

Father, I need your help. My heart is weary and tired. Heal the weariness with refreshment and peace. Show me how. Amen.

Jesus, you are the one who can save us and all mankind. Jesus, save! Amen.

Father, when I look at you, I see love. Help me give this love to everyone. Amen.

Jesus, all of us have a task to do. It is to love. Help us love. Amen. Father, we need the truth in our world. Help us to hear truth, to know truth, and to speak truth. Amen.

Father, heal the wounds and set us free—free from all bitterness, revenge, and unkindness. Help us put aside the differences and the hurts and make us live in your peace, your love, and your joy. Amen. Father, I do not do as I should. Help me. Amen.

Father, I place this intention in your heart. Free this person from all anxiety, worry, and fear. Let them live in your peace. Amen.

Father, this situation needs your help. I ask for your help. Amen. Jesus, you came to help us and to show us the way to live our lives in your love and peace. Give us this peace. Amen.

"Thank God for His marvelous love, for His miracle mercy to the children He loves" (Ps. 107:8).

Thank you for your love, kind Father. Amen.

Father, I pray for truth in my life. Amen.

Father, there is only you, Lord, for us to be saved! Amen.

Jesus, I love you. Amen.

Father, the world is in chaos. Heal, deliver, change, and save the whole world. Amen.

Jesus, I pray for the world to know *you*, love *you*, and serve *you*. Amen.

Jesus, there is no other name by which we can be saved. Save us now, dear Jesus, in *your name*. Amen!

Father, I unite my prayers with all of those who are praying with me. Hear us, kind Father, for all of these needs and those of the ones who have asked for our prayers. Amen.

Rejoice before the Lord, your God.

Jesus, help this situation. I pray for truth. Thank you, Jesus. Amen.

Dear Father, help me. I need your help! Amen.

Father, there is so much that I need to pray for. Help me pray. Amen.
Jesus, the way is not clear. Make it clear. Amen.

Father, help all of those that I said I would pray for. Help them all!
Amen.

Jesus, help us to be safe. Help our families to be safe. Help us *all* to
be *safe*. Amen.

Jesus, the way is dark. Show us the way to the light. Amen.

Father, you are my joy, rest, hope, life, love, and dream to do better.
Amen.

PART 6

"BEHOLD, I BRING YOU TIDINGS OF GREAT JOY, WHICH SHALL BE TO ALL THE PEOPLES. A SAVIOR IS BORN WHO IS CHRIST THE LORD."

Reading to a child is one of the most wonderful pastimes. Spending time together with children and sharing stories with them leave wonderful memories in both the child and the reader. It is a time that will live on in the memories of both. This is a gift that we give to children, and this special story is one of them.

PREFACE

A few years ago, I was asked to plan a Christmas program for our children's group at church. I decided to have the Christmas story narrated while the children acted out the various parts. I divided the parts among the different age groups. The three-to-four-year-old age group would portray little sheep, and they had the most adorable costumes. My little four-year-old neighbor, Jasmine, was in that group. After the first practice, Jasmine came to me and "announced" that she did not want to be a sheep, but she wanted to be an angel. I explained to her that an older class would portray angels. So she refused to be in the program if she couldn't be one of the angels. I tried to reason with her—as did the other teachers, the group leader, and her grandmother—but to no avail.

I thought I would take a different approach and try to show her how special it was to be part of the first group to know of Jesus's birth. So I sat down at my kitchen table and started writing about a little lamb named Jazzy who by some "coincidence" took on a few of the traits of Jasmine's personality.

When the story was finished, I took it next door and read it to Jasmine.

After I finished, she had a big smile on her face and decided it would be pretty special to be a lamb after all.

JAZZY AND THE SHINY, BRIGHT NIGHT

Lynda Cross Slowikowski

Many, many years ago—in a land far, far away—there lived a little lamb named Jazzy. Jazzy was a new lamb, and she was part of a big flock of sheep. They lived on a hillside just outside of a small village called Bethlehem. Jazzy always tried to be a good little lamb and stay close to her mama and listen to the shepherds who took care of them. But sometimes, as hard as she tried, Jazzy didn't do exactly what she was supposed to do. It seemed that the shepherds always had to take special care of Jazzy. She was a very curious little lamb, and sometimes she would wander away from the rest of the flock so she could see some of the amazing things that were around the hillside. Sometimes she would see pretty flowers or trees. One time, she noticed a little cave and peeked inside the opening. It looked very dark inside the cave. Even though the shepherds always found Jazzy when she wandered away, and even though she was a very brave and curious little lamb, she was afraid that the shepherds wouldn't be able to find her if she went into the cave. So Jazzy stayed away from the cave. Sometimes when it was raining, Jazzy's hoofs would get all muddy, and that would make it hard for her to walk. When the shepherds found her, they would wipe her feet and then say, "Jazzy, Jazzy! You need to stay close to our flocks and to your mama!"

In her own language, Jazzy said "Baaaaaaa" and promised the shepherds that she would try very hard to do as they said.

Late one night, after a big day of adventures, Jazzy cuddled up with the other sheep to rest for the night. All of a sudden, something very big and wonderful happened. The sky lit up with a bright light, and Jazzy saw someone in the sky. Even though she had never seen one before, she just knew she was seeing an angel. The shepherds were very afraid, but not Jazzy! She was excited and, of course, curious about the angel.

Soon the angel started to talk to the shepherds and told them not to be afraid because in the little village of Bethlehem, a child had been born who was sent to be the savior of the world. Jazzy had heard the shepherds often talk about how they and their people had been waiting for many, many years for a king to come to help them. Jazzy figured that if the angel took the time to come from heaven to tell the shepherds about the baby, then this baby must be the king that everyone had been waiting for!

Then the angel told the shepherds that they would find the baby wrapped in cloths and lying in a manger in a stable in the village. Jazzy thought it was very strange that a king would be born in a stable instead of in a big and beautiful palace, but she figured that if the angel said that was how it was, then it must be true! All of a sudden, something very amazing happened. The angel was joined in the sky by many angels!

The light from the angels was so bright, it was like daytime instead of night! The angels started to sing together: "Glory to God in the highest heaven and peace on earth!"

All of a sudden, the sky was dark again! The angels were gone! Jazzy felt so sad because she really loved looking at the beautiful angels and hearing their song! She looked around and saw the shepherds whispering to one another. Because she was a brave and curious lamb, she quietly came close to the shepherds to hear what they were saying.

The shepherds decided to leave the flock for a little while and go into the village of Bethlehem and try to find the baby that the angels told them about. She knew the shepherds wouldn't let her go along with them, but there was no way that Jazzy was going to stay behind! So when the shepherds started to go toward Bethlehem, Jazzy quietly followed them. She stayed far enough behind them so that they couldn't see her, but she could still see them. Once in a while, one of the shepherds would turn around! It was almost as if he knew that they were being followed! Whenever that happened, Jazzy would quickly hide behind a rock or a bush or even a tree! Soon they were entering the tiny town of Bethlehem. The shepherds kept walking and passed many houses and inns. There were so many doorways and other places for Jazzy to hide so the shepherds wouldn't know that she had followed them. Finally, the shepherds stopped outside of a stable. Jazzy peeked around the corner to see why the shepherds had stopped and wondered what they were seeing.

Then Jazzy saw a wonderful sight! In the middle of the stable and on a bed of hay, there was a tiny baby boy! There were other animals in the stable and even some sheep!

This must be the king that the angels talked about, Jazzy thought.

The shepherds knew it too because they bowed down in front of the manger to worship the baby. The baby's mother told the shepherds that the baby's name was Jesus. Even though the baby couldn't see her— because she was hiding, of course—Jazzy knew that the baby loved her.

After the shepherds had worshipped their king, they decided that it was time for them to go back and tend to their flock. Jazzy was still watching the baby, and when the shepherds turned around, they saw her! She was so afraid that the shepherds would be angry with her for leaving her mama and the flock to follow them. Jazzy was so surprised. The shepherds looked down and smiled at her. One of them picked her up and carried her back to the Bethlehem hillside. After they got back to the flock, Jazzy lay down beside her mama.

She promised herself in her own special language that she would try to be a very good lamb so the shepherds wouldn't have to go away from the flock to find her. She knew that was what the baby would want her to do! Jazzy closed her eyes and fell asleep, dreaming of the shiny, bright night when she got to see the special baby who was the king of the world!

A PLAY FOR CHILDREN
TO PERFORM

A LIGHT FOR THE NATIONS

Carolyn Bradley

(Mary is seated, holding her baby, Jesus, in her arms.)

Mary:
"What will you be, little boy?
What will you be? Will you be a star
shining in the night— A light for truth?
What will you be?"

(Joseph enters.)

Joseph:
"Mary, there are shepherds coming.
I hear the bleating of the sheep.

Mary:
"Why are they here, Joseph?"

Joseph:
"It must be the baby."

(Shepherds enter.)

First Shepherd:
"We have come to see the baby.
He is tiny. He is small. But *look*!

251

Out there—*angels*! We saw *angels*
In the sky—over there!"

(First Shepherd points his finger to the direction.)

Second Shepherd: "They were singing praises to God:
                        'Glory to God in the highest!
                        Glory to God!'"

Mary: "What did they say?"

Third Shepherd: "They said a child was born
                        in a manger— a savior who is Christ the
                        Lord. "'You will find the baby wrapped
                        in swaddling clothes.
                        A manger—a manger is his bed.'"

Joseph: "Sleep, little baby, sleep.
                        He is sleeping, Mary."

Scripture Reader: Isaiah 42:1–7
                        "Here is my servant.
                        I have made him strong.
                        He is my chosen one.
                        I am pleased with him.
                        I have given him my Spirit,
                        And he will bring justice to the nations.
                        He won't shout or yell or
                        call out in the streets.
                        He won't break off a bent reed
                        Or put out a dying flame,
                        But he will make sure that

justice is done.
He won't quit or give up
Until he brings justice everywhere
on earth
And people everywhere long for
his teaching.
I am the Lord God. I created the heavens
Like an open tent above.
I made the earth and everything
that grows on it.
I am the source of life for
all who live on this earth,
So listen to what I say.
I chose you to bring justice,
and I am here at your side.
I selected and sent you to bring light
And my promise of hope to the nations.
You will give sight to the blind.
You will set prisoners free
from dark dungeons."

Joseph: "Mary, it is the child!"
                           The child is Emmanuel—the Savior—
                           The Christ—
                           A light to the nations."

(Mary looks over to the side.)

Joseph: "Mary, what is it?"

Mary: "Joseph, the words—
                           He will be a light. *See* the light."

(Mary points to the light.)

(An angel enters.)

Angel: "I have a crown—a crown for the baby.
                    It is a crown he must wear."

Mary: "Why are there thorns?
                    Roses with thorns?"

Angel: "Little baby, little light,
                    Thorns will pierce your brow,
                    Lashes will beat upon your back,
                    and nail prints will mar your hands.
                    A cross will be your bed to lie upon."

(Mary sighs.)

Mary: "Little baby, did you know?
                    He sleeps, Joseph. He sleeps."

Joseph: "Look, Mary. He opens his eyes.

                    Is there a tear?"

Mary: "Oh, no, Joseph. It is a smile!"

THE HOLLY BERRIES

(Santa Claus enters.)

Children:	"Santa Claus! Santa Claus!"
Santa:	"Hello, children. I have come to tell you a very special story."
Children:	"What story, Santa?"
Santa:	"It is a story of love— the greatest love the world has ever known."
Children:	"Tell us about it, Santa."
Santa:	"The holly is a symbol of Christmas. The red berries stand for love."
Children:	"Whose love, Santa?"
Santa:	"Sit down, children. Gather around me."

(Children sit down in a semicircle.)

"A long time ago, there was a star-filled night over Bethlehem, and angels were in the sky, telling shepherds of a newborn *king*. It is Jesus, children. The shepherds were told to go to Bethlehem—to a stable— where they would find the baby in a manger."

Children: "What happened then, Santa?"

Santa: "The shepherds found the baby.
                    He was lying in a manger—
                    just as the angels had said."

Children: "What did they do, Santa?"

Santa: "They told Mary, his mother, about the
                    angels telling them to go there and see
                    the *baby*. He is the *Savior*, children,
                    for the angels said,
                    'Fear not, for I bring you tidings of great
                    joy, for unto you, in the city of
                    Bethlehem is born a Savior who
                    is Christ the Lord.'"

Children: "Why did he come?"

Santa: "He came to save the world from sin—
                    so that all people would be saved.
                    He came to save you."

Children:	"What a beautiful story, Santa!"
Santa:	"*There is more, children.* Jesus came to save. Years later, that same baby would be grown and die on a cross for us— for you and for me. He would die to shed the last drop of his blood, like the holly berries so red, for all of us. He died to give us love— the greatest love there ever was! I carry on that love at Christmas. Whenever we give love, we give the gift of Jesus to one another. When you open your presents on Christmas Day, remember the love. It is in each package. *Christmas is love— the love of Jesus for us all!*"

(Children gather around Santa, and all sing a Christmas carol together.)

"*We wish you a Merry Christmas, we wish you a Merry Christmas, we wish you a Merry Christmas, and a Happy New Year.*"

www.ingramcontent.com/pod-product-compliance
Lightning Source LLC
Chambersburg PA
CBHW022251251125
35994CB00038B/367